Honorable Treason

Also by David Freeman Hawke

In the Midst of a Revolution (1961)

American Colloquy (co-editor with Leonard Lief, 1963)

*A Transaction of Free Men: The Birth and Course of
the Declaration of Independence* (1964)

The Colonial Experience (1966)

U.S. Colonial History: Readings and Documents (editor, 1966)

American History Landmarks (editor, six volumes, 1970–1972)

Benjamin Rush: Revolutionary Gadfly (1971)

Paine (1974)

Benjamin Franklin: What Manner of Man? (1976)

Honorable Treason

The Declaration of Independence and the Men Who Signed It

David Freeman Hawke

The Viking Press · New York

To Liadain
Matthew and
Samantha

First published in 1976 by The Viking Press, Inc.
625 Madison Avenue, New York, N.Y. 10022

Published simultaneously in Canada by
The Macmillan Company of Canada Limited

LIBRARY OF CONGRESS CATALOGING IN PUBLICATION DATA
Hawke, David Freeman.
    Honorable treason.

    Bibliography: p.
    Includes index.
    1. United States.   Declaration of independence.
2. United States.   Declaration of independence—
                    Signers.   I. Title.
    E221.H25   973.3'13'0922   75-30968
                    ISBN 0-670-37857-7

Printed in U.S.A.

Author's Note

In 1964 I published *A Transaction of Free Men: The Birth and Course of the Declaration of Independence.* That book, I thought, revealed all I had to say on the Declaration and the men who made it. I turned to other matters. Sometime later, while doing a biography of Benjamin Rush, I came upon a remark of John Adams that unsettled me. "The Declaration of Independence I always considered as a theatrical show," Adams said thirty-five years after he and his friend Rush had signed the document. "Jefferson ran away with all the stage effect of that . . . and all the glory of it." Adams had a point. The bulk of the glory had gone to Jefferson. My own study had, except for John Adams, ignored most of the other gentlemen who shared in the momentous decision to break all ties with Great Britain. I determined to rectify the oversight with a book of sketches that would give each of the fifty-six Signers his day in the sun.

The book began as a lighthearted venture. It would be a collection of "profiles"—the facts of the Signers' lives could easily be found in the *Dictionary of American Biography.* It would picture each of these gentlemen as his colleagues saw him. The imposing John Witherspoon, for instance, was a renowned Presbyterian minister and president of the College of New Jersey (now Princeton University), but his fellow delegates did not seem to have an especially high regard for him, partly because it made them uneasy to have a clergyman in their midst. Anecdotes would be used to reveal the human side of men who have come down to us through John Trumbull's famous painting as bewigged, stiff, and solemn-faced. Benjamin Franklin would become a less remote figure, I hoped, when he revealed that he liked to shave himself because it allowed him to avoid the "dull razors, and dirty fingers or bad breath of a slovenly barber."

Although I had worked nearly twenty years in the field of eighteenth-century American history, I began the research knowing little about any of the Signers except the most famous. Most upon acquaintance turned out to be pleasant surprises. The now largely forgotten Abraham Clark of New Jersey emerged as perhaps the single home-grown radical in Congress, although his colleagues regarded him largely as an exasperating hair shirt. Caesar Rodney of Delaware comes through in his letters as a somewhat solemn, even pompous gentleman, but to his colleagues he was an adroit politician and a man of good humor, adept at relieving tension with a joke or an anecdote when a debate heated up. Richard Henry Lee has come down as one of the leaders in the fight for independence, but fellow delegates had a higher opinion of his amiable, lesser known brother Francis Lightfoot Lee.

Midway through the book I noticed that when a Signer's life reached early 1776 the sketch acquired something of the solemnity found in Trumbull's painting of the signing of the Declaration. Suddenly it struck me that two events had occurred in January 1776 to change the delegates' mood. That month the members learned that the king, who earlier had branded them rebellious traitors, now accused them of seeking to establish "an independent empire" in America. Almost simultaneously with the arrival of this news there "burst from the press" a pamphlet by Thomas Paine. It was entitled *Common Sense* and urged America to fulfill the king's prediction. Up to now the bulk of Congress had opposed independence; only a small minority favored it. From early January on every member saw the question could no longer be dodged. As each man during the ensuing six months agonized over his decision, both he and Congress changed. Tempers became shorter, debates more heated. Some delegates were so tortured by the issue they became physically ill. Some, to avoid a decision, left Congress. But the majority resolutely, day after day, pondered the question, listening to the arguments for and against independence, querying friends at home for their opinions, while they inched their way, each by a private route, toward a decision. Slowly, painfully, men who had earlier often appeared timid or petty on great issues, or bound by prejudices of their region or colony, opened their minds and rose above their provincial backgrounds. Each knew the great risk he took if he voted for independence. Posterity might profit by his decision, but he stood to gain little for himself and to lose much.

Slowly, too, it dawned on me that it is one thing to chip away at the crust on the monuments of the Founding Fathers, to attempt to make them more human, but something else to treat cavalierly men who dared to declare their colonies free and independent from the most powerful nation in the western world. Such men cannot be treated lightly. These fifty-six gentlemen made their decision behind closed doors, but when the time came to pledge their lives, their fortunes, and their sacred honor, they did so publicly, putting their names on the Declaration of Independence where all the world could read them.

Contents

Honorable Treason

1

A Momentous Question

The Pennsylvania State House lay on the western outskirts of Philadelphia, along Chestnut Street between Fifth and Sixth. Aside from its size, which was imposing for the day, it blended perfectly into the surroundings. It was built of the same light-red brick used throughout the city and designed in the clean, plain style that satisfied Quakers "as the least expensive, but also the most neat and commodious." The king's arms hung over the main entrance through which delegates to the Second Continental Congress stepped each morning.

Above the building rose a squat tower "of such miserable architecture, that the legislature have wisely determined to let it go to decay (the upper part being entirely of wood) that it may hereafter be built upon a new and more elegant construction." The tower housed a large bell and the works for the two clock dials hanging beneath the eaves of the east and west outer walls. Probably not one in a hundred Philadelphians could have told a visitor that the bell bore a

Biblical inscription appropriate for this day, June 7, 1776. It read: "Proclaim liberty throughout all the land unto all the inhabitants thereof."

Behind the State House a large yard, surrounded by a brick wall seven feet high, stretched southward to Walnut Street. Here members of Congress often strolled for a smoke or to relax from their long, tedious sessions. A tavern conveniently located across Chestnut Street probably to some degree influenced the conduct of business within the first-floor chamber of the State House where the Second Congress met.

It was the day Congress would be asked to declare the United Colonies free and independent states. Richard Henry Lee would be remembered as the man who on this clear and balmy morning introduced the resolution calling for this momentous decision, but the day really belonged to Samuel Adams of Massachusetts. The character of Samuel Adams, his cousin John Adams once remarked, "will never be accurately known to posterity, as it never was sufficiently known to its own age; his merit in the Revolution, if there was any merit in it, was and is beyond all calculation."

Samuel Adams
AGE: 53   POLITICIAN

Five years later nearly all who had signed the Declaration were gone from Congress. Several had died, a few had been sent abroad for the new nation, most had retired to private life or accepted posts in their state governments. But Samuel Adams still sat in Congress, keeping an eye on the crusade he more than any man had launched well over a decade earlier. To the new generation of younger politicians who now surrounded him he looked harmless, hardly "that Machiavel of Chaos" the English ministry had called him—a plain man, plainly dressed, no stouter now than he had been as a youth, his hair gray, his hands captive to a palsy that kept them constantly trembling. He "has a pretty general knowledge of [congressional] affairs and is particularly attentive to everything that affects his own state or friends," one of the newcomers observed. "He is neither eloquent nor talkative; but having the full command of his passions, and possessing a great deal of caution and court cunning he is well fitted for a politician in every case where great and good abilities are not requisite."

Others who had worked with him earlier in Congress might have questioned whether he lacked "great and good abilities," but no one doubted that Adams was a flawed man. He *was* parochial. He "would have the state of Massachusetts govern the nation," a friendly acquaintance said, "the town of Boston govern Massachusetts, and that he should govern the town of Boston, and then the whole would not be intentionally ill-governed." He dispensed a naïve prescription for curing America's ills. "If the youth are carefully educated, if the principles of morality are strongly inculcated," he said, good government would naturally result. "Bigotry and narrowness" tinged both his religion and politics, said another who admired him. "He was a strict Calvinist; and probably no individual of his day had so much of the feelings of the ancient Puritans as he possessed." He could be vindictive beyond belief. He trusted no man and had no intimate friends. He lied, or at best twisted facts, to suit his purpose. He was a jealous man. He ceased speaking to John Hancock when his onetime protégé deviated from a path Adams thought he should travel. A coolness set in when his closest ally, distant cousin John Adams, surpassed him in reputation among members of Congress. He was an inflexible man. "I am *in* fashion and *out* of fashion, as the whim goes," he once said. "I will stand alone; I will oppose tyranny at the threshold, though the fabric fall and I perish in its ruins." Samuel Adams did not change. The times and men did. The oncoming generation in 1781 found him out of fashion; in 1776 he was in fashion, at least among those eager for independence. "A truly great man, wise in council, fertile in resources, immovable in his purpose," Jefferson said. "I always considered him, more than any other member, the *fountain* of our more important measures," and, he added, "truly the *Man of the Revolution.*"

Samuel Adams had been reared in comfortable circumstances. His father owned a malt house and had invested the modest profits wisely enough to accumulate a small fortune. The son went to Harvard, class of 1740. From there, his mother hoped he would move on into the church. Instead, he studied law for a while but dropped it, then worked for a merchant who dropped him. His father gave him £1000 to set up a business; Samuel lost half of it in a loan to an impecunious friend. Meanwhile the long-suffering father was unwittingly training his son for politics. At meetings of the Caucus Club, an informal gathering of club-house politicians, Samuel learned how his father and his cronies manipulated the Boston town meeting.

When he was twenty-one he won his first political post in an election probably managed by his father. The office, clerk of the market, was of no importance except as a training ground for a neophyte politician. Two years later his father died, leaving behind a mountain of debts. He had invested heavily in a land-bank scheme that the government put out of business. The sheriff, prodded by creditors of the defunct bank, moved in to attach the malt business. Samuel threatened "to prosecute in the law any person whomsoever who shall trespass upon that estate." Right was not on his side, but his noise intimidated the "oppressors"; they backed off, and Adams held on to the malt business. Not that he made much of it. He preferred to concentrate on politics. His first coup came when he was elected collector of taxes for Boston. Competently handled, the post could have brought in a decent income. But Adams was lax about collections and by 1765 so far behind that he owed the town £8000. The town sued for payment and won the case in court, but by then Samuel Adams controlled the town meeting and nothing more came of the matter.

Samuel Adams first came into fashion with the Stamp Act in 1765, when he was forty-three years old and had done nothing worth boasting about. The Stamp Act taxed virtually all paper that circulated in America—newspapers, pamphlets, almanacs, writs, licenses, bills of lading, bonds, deeds, indentures, leases, contracts. The list seemed endless. Adams railed against the act through the press and from a seat in the legislature. He probably masterminded and certainly approved of the riots in which the house of Thomas Hutchinson, currently lieutenant governor of the colony, was looted. Repeal of the Stamp Act in 1766 did not appease him. He warned that nothing could redeem a government corrupt beyond redemption. The land must be cleansed of evil, and when the Townshend duties came he urged "the disuse of foreign superfluities" that were corrupting the American spirit. In a circular letter drafted by him and sent to all colonial legislatures he called for united action against British oppression. When British troops were brought into Boston to keep peace he concocted a *Journal of Events* that gave a weekly summary of wrongs perpetrated by the soldiers and sent it to newspapers up and down the coast. The local leader had by now become a politician with a continental reputation.

The troops in Boston infuriated Adams. "If you are men, behave like men," he told the people; "let us take up arms immediately, and be free, and seize all the king's officers." He professed to be no friend to riot or tumult, "but when the people are oppressed, when their rights are infringed, when their property is invaded," they must "boldly assert their freedom; and they are to be justified in so doing." One winter night a platoon of soldiers provoked by a mob killed five citizens. The Boston Massacre, as Adams made sure it was called, became the centerpiece in his display of British atrocities. But words that once stirred, techniques that once worked, now fell flat, and, with the repeal of all the Townshend duties but the one on tea, people went back to using "foreign superfluities." John Hancock and John Adams abandoned the crusade, and for the next two years Samuel Adams worked virtually alone. He wrote some forty essays that alerted the people to the slightest infringement of their rights, but the people continued placidly about their business. By November 1772 he was losing his hold over the Boston town meeting—he barely managed re-election to the House of Representatives that month —but by ingenious maneuvering he got it to authorize the creation of a committee of correspondence, whose purpose would be "to state the rights of the colonists and of this province in particular, as men, as Christians, and as subjects; and to communicate the same to the several towns and to the world." He now had the machinery to crank up a revolution; he only needed something to feed into the machinery. We cannot make events, he once said. "Our business is wisely to improve upon them."

The first chance of improvement came when Benjamin Franklin sent over from England a packet of stolen letters, several of which were written by Thomas Hutchinson. Franklin sent them for Adams and his friends to read but not to copy or to publish. With the connivance of Hancock, now back in the fold, Adams edited the letters and saw them printed in every important newspaper in the colonies. The correspondence revealed little Hutchinson had not said publicly, but Adams' explication of their contents destroyed the governor's reputation. The arrival from London of ships loaded with tea offered another event to be improved upon. After the Boston Tea Party Adams dared to predict that if Britain did "not return to the principles of moderation and equity," she would bring on *the entire separation and independence of the colonies.*" Later he admitted that independence "had been the first wish of his heart seven years before the war."

Adams wanted to revive the boycott against British goods, but Boston had moved too boldly and leaders elsewhere hung back. The destruction of private property did not excite admiration in other colonies. But when Parliament sought to starve Boston into submission by closing her port to all traffic, displeasure turned to sympathy. The precedent of punishing a city for the action of a mob could not be countenanced. While the continent fed supplies into Boston by land a call went out to discuss the crisis at an intercolonial congress which would meet in Philadelphia.

No one in Boston, so enemies said, excelled Samuel Adams in duplicity. "He could transform his self into an Angel of Light with the weak religionist," according to one man, "and with the abandoned he would disrobe his self and appear with his cloven foot and in his native blackness of darkness." The Angel of Light took the stage at the First Continental Congress. At the opening session someone suggested the meeting might begin with a prayer. John Jay of New York opposed the motion "because we were so divided in religious sentiments." Samuel Adams, as his cousin John recalled the speech, rose and said, "he was no bigot, and could hear a prayer from a gentleman of piety and virtue, who was at the same time a friend to his country. He was a stranger in Philadelphia, but had heard that Mr. Duché (Dushay they pronounce it) deserved that character, and therefore he moved that Mr. Duché, an Episcopal clergyman, might be desired to read prayers to the Congress tomorrow morning." That ecumenical appeal from a rigid Congregationalist astonished the assembly. From that moment Adams had the delegates in hand, or enough of them to obtain from Congress all he wanted. He may be unremarkable "for brilliant abilities," said Joseph Galloway of Pennsylvania, himself a supreme politician, but he is "equal to most men in popular intrigue and the management of a faction. He eats little, sleeps little, thinks much, and is most decisive and indefatigable in the pursuit of his objects."

In the Second Congress he worked as before, only now openly for independence. No man had welcomed the battle at Lexington more than he. "This day is a glorious day for America," he said. He told an acquaintance that "if it were revealed to him that nine hundred and ninety-nine Americans out of one thousand would perish in a war for liberty, he would vote for that war, rather than see his country enslaved. The survivors in such a war, though few, would propagate a nation of freemen."

He cultivated talent for the cause in Philadelphia as he had in Boston. "My high reverence for Samuel Adams was returned by habitual notices from him which highly flattered me," said Jefferson. He spoke seldom from the floor, and when he did it was, though to the point and clearly, in a "hesitating, grunting" manner made even more distracting by the trembling hands. He shunned committee work, preferring to manipulate affairs off stage. Few important committee assignments, however, were made without consulting him, and no major debate occurred for which he did not plan the program of speakers for his side of the argument. He was, Jefferson said, "constantly holding caucuses of distinguished men (among whom was R. H. Lee) at which the generality of the measures pursued were previously determined on, and at which the parts were assigned to the different actors, who afterwards appeared in them."

On June 6, 1776, Samuel Adams hinted in a letter to a friend what the morrow held for America. "I have long wished for the determination of some momentous questions," he wrote, putting his thoughts obliquely for fear that if the British intercepted the letter they might get wind of what was brewing in Congress. "If delay shall prove mischievous I shall have no reason to reflect upon myself; everyone here knows what my sentiments have been. However, tomorrow a motion will be made, and a question I hope decided, the most important that was ever agitated in America. I have no doubt but it will be decided to *your* satisfaction. This being done, things will go on in the right channel and our country will be saved. The bearer awaits. Adieu."

2

The Colossus

"Patience! Patience! Patience!" John Adams once said during the early days of the Revolution to a friend who wanted to make the world over in a day. Patience is the "first, the last and the middle virtue of a politician."

In the summer of 1776 such advice from John Adams sounded strange to John Dickinson of Pennsylvania, who considered patience the one virtue his colleague from Massachusetts lacked. The two had argued for a year about independence. "What is the reason, Mr. Adams, that you New Englandmen oppose our measures of reconciliation?" Dickinson had asked one afternoon in July 1775. "Look ye! If you don't concur with us in our pacific system, I and a number of us will break off from you in New England, and we will carry on the opposition by ourselves in our own way."

Adams knew his colleagues could make good the threat to break apart the fragile union of the colonies. If he led the Pennsylvania delegation from Congress, probably New York would follow, and in their wake New Jersey, Maryland, and

Delaware. The vision angered Adams. "A certain great fortune and piddling genius, whose fame has been trumpeted so loudly, has given a silly cast to our whole doings," he wrote in a letter of Dickinson. The British captured the letter and published it. For months thereafter Adams was "an object of nearly universal detestation" who walked the streets of Philadelphia alone, snubbed by colleagues in Congress and "all the moderate and prudent people in America," who did not take lightly any public censure of their hero John Dickinson.

Adams learned from the experience to practice the patience he preached. Publicly he no longer talked of independence. Privately he told friends that the Massachusetts delegation in Congress, for all its desire to force a break from Britain, must control its tongue. Sometimes he likened the thirteen colonies to a convoy of ships that must be kept in line; sometimes to a horse-drawn coach where "the swiftest horses must be slackened and the slowest quickened, that all may keep an even pace"; sometimes to a house filled with thirteen clocks that must be timed to strike together. Regardless of how he put it, the point came through—independence could not be declared until all thirteen "ships," "horses," or "clocks" moved as one.

That the colonies eventually voted unanimously for independence owed as much to John Adams as to any man in Congress. "Every member of Congress in 1776 acknowledged him to be the first man in the House," his friend Benjamin Rush said. "Dr. Brownson of Georgia used to say when he spoke he fancied an angel was let down from heaven to illumine the Congress. He saw the whole of a subject at a single glance, and by a happy union of the powers of reasoning and persuasion often succeeded in carrying measures which were at first sight of an unpopular nature."

According to Thomas Jefferson, John Adams played "very little part" in Samuel Adams' strategy-planning caucuses, "but as one of the actors in the measures decided on in them, he was a *Colossus.*" He hardly looked the part. He was a stumpy man—no taller than five feet six inches—with a balding head and a thickening paunch. When asked by an artist to describe himself, he said good humoredly, "John . . . should be painted looking like a short thick archbishop of Canterbury, seated at the table with a pen in his hand."

John Adams

AGE: 40   LAWYER

Adams was born in Braintree, Massachusetts, the son of a farmer who came from a long line of farmers with roots deep in the history of Massachusetts. He entered Harvard, class of 1755, when he was fifteen. As the eldest son, he was expected to be the family's tithe to the church. He graduated the year of Braddock's defeat in western Pennsylvania, an event that led him to predict that "if we can remove the turbulent Gallicks . . . the only way to keep us from setting up for ourselves is to disunite us."

Adams left college uncertain of what he wanted to do with his life. To gain time for thought he took a stopgap position as a teacher in the back-country village of Worcester, some sixty miles west of Boston. He had about fifty students, "a large number of little runtlings, just capable of lisping A,B, C and troubling the master." A friend thought "cultivating and pruning these tender plants" could be a rewarding occupation. Adams doubted it and said that "to keep this school any length of time would make a base weed and ignoble shrub of me."

But the runtlings had to be endured until he settled on a career. After much thought he rejected the ministry. "As far as I can observe, people are not disposed to inquire for piety, integrity, good sense, or learning in a young preacher, but for stupidity," he said. Against the advice of friends and family he finally chose to study law. He did not then think much of the legal profession —"a fumbling and raking amidst the rubbish of writs, indictments, pleas . . . that have neither harmony nor meaning"—but it offered a young man from a middling background a chance to prosper. "Necessity drove me to this determination," he said, "but my inclination, I think, was to preach." He read in the office of a local lawyer for two years while continuing to teach the runtlings of Worcester. With the end of the apprenticeship he headed immediately for Braintree. "I panted for want of the breezes from the sea, and the pure zephyrs from the rocky mountains of my native town."

A lawyer in Boston who arranged for his admission to the bar offered several pieces of advice. "One is, to pursue the study of law, rather than the gain of it; pursue the gain of it enough to keep out of the briers, but give your main attention to the study of it. The next is, not to marry early; for an early marriage will obstruct your improvement; and in the next place, it will involve you in expense. Another thing is, not to keep much company, for the application of a man who aims to be a lawyer must be incessant; his attention to his books must be constant, which is inconsistent with keeping much company."

Adams listened to these admonitions and determined to follow them, though his diary recounted a string of failures to live up to the mark. The sun regularly caught him abed. "I have smoked, chatted, trifled, loitered away this whole day almost," went one entry, "in unloading a cart, in cutting oven wood, in making and recruiting my own fire, in eating victuals and apples, in drinking tea, cutting and smoking tobacco, and in chatting with Dr. Savil's wife at their house and this." But other entries show he was satisfying a resolve made when he was admitted to the bar—to "aim at an exact knowledge of nature, end, and means of government; compare the different forms of it with each other, and each of them with their effects on public and private happiness."

He had plenty time for reading, for little business came his way. Possibly, he thought, the fault lay with himself. "I have been very negligent and faulty in not treating Deacon S——, Nat B——, Deacon B——, etc., with more attention and sprightliness," he said. He cautioned himself that to promote a career "popularity, next to virtue and wisdom, ought to be aimed at." He warned himself that "reputation ought to be the perpetual subject of my thoughts, and aim of my behavior. How shall I gain a reputation! I feel vexed, fretted, chafed; the thought of no business mortifies me. But let me banish these fears; let me assume a fortitude, a greatness of mind."

He soon decided the fault lay less with him than the village of Braintree, a place too small for a young man on the make. He moved to Boston, only to be overwhelmed by the distractions. "Who can study in Boston streets?" he grumbled. "My eyes are so diverted with chimney-sweepers, sawyers of wood, merchants, ladies, priests, carts, horses, oxen, coaches, marketmen and women, soldiers, sailors; and my ears with the rattle-gabble of them all, that I cannot think long enough in the street upon any one thing to start and pursue a thought." The death of his father two years later carried him back to Braintree to live with his mother. The town meeting elected him surveyor of the highways. He went at the job with his usual vigor, inquiring of neighboring towns their "methods of mending highways by a rate" and set up a system that lasted for over a half century. When he got the town to limit to three the taverns permitted to serve alcohol—taverns for him were "the eternal haunt of loose, disorderly people," dens where "diseases, vicious habits, bastards, and legislators are frequently begotten"—he learned his first major lesson in politics and patience. "I am creating enemies in every quarter," he said when trying to enforce the town ordinance. "I shall have the ill will of the whole town. . . . This will not do."

Adams turned from reform to building up a law practice, cultivating popularity, and making money. He needed money now, for he had fallen in love with Abigail Smith. The courtship lasted four years; her parents did not think John Adams good enough for their daughter. It was an ordeal for both. Once when a snowstorm kept them from meeting, Adams said it was just as well, for "aches, aches, agues and repentance might be the consequence of a contact in present circumstances." Sometimes they sparred. He told her she lacked a "stately strut," crossed her legs when sitting, hung her head "like a bulrush." She told him "a gentleman has no business to concern himself about the legs of a lady." Finally, late in 1764, they married; he was then twenty-nine, she some ten years younger. The next year he reported in his diary that "1765 has been the most remarkable year of my life." Married life delighted him, he had picked up several clients in a tour of the court circuit, and been charmed by America's reaction to the Stamp Act.

The Stamp Act itself embittered him. Lawyers' refusal to buy the special stamps the act required for all legal documents caused the courts to be closed. "I have not drawn a writ since the first of November," Adams said. "I was but just getting into my gears, just getting under sail, and an embargo is laid upon the ship. . . . I have . . . groped in dark obscurity, till of late, and had but just become and gained a small degree of reputation, when this execrable project was set on foot for my ruin as well as that of America in general, and of Great Britain."

The Stamp Act carried Adams from local into provincial politics. He published a pamphlet attacking the act as contrary to the rights of man, "*rights* that cannot be repealed or restrained by human laws—*rights* derived from the great Legislator of the universe." In a set of instructions for Braintree's representative in the legislature he attacked the act as "burthensome," unconstitutional, and an "alarming extension of the power of the Courts of Admiralty." Within a year the Stamp Act was repealed, the courts were reopened in Massachusetts, and Adams found himself traveling the circuit, only now as one of the colony's leading lawyers. In order to deal more easily with his enlarged practice he moved back to Boston. When the customhouse sued John Hancock for treble the value of an illegal cargo of wine carried aboard his sloop *Liberty*, Hancock hired Adams to defend him. "A painful drudgery I had of his cause," Adams recalled. "There were few days through the whole winter when I was not summoned to attend the Court of Admiralty." When the government finally dropped charges, Adams was "weary and disgusted" with the case, the court, "and even the tyrannical bell that dongled me out of my house every morning." Another case, in which he defended four sailors charged with murdering an officer of the royal navy who tried to impress them, pleased him more. He unearthed a statute that prohibited impressment in America. A reluctant court accepted his argument of "justifiable homicide" and set the sailors free. A third case gave the greatest satisfaction but nearly ruined him. He agreed in the interest of justice to serve as defense counsel for the British officer and soldiers who, in March 1770, had perpetrated the so-called Boston Massacre. Officer and men were acquitted or let off with minor sentences, although only partly through Adams' legal skill. Five members of the jury did business with the British army and were predisposed toward the accused before they heard the case. Adams considered his role "one of the most gallant, generous, manly and disinterested actions of my whole life, and one of the best pieces of service I ever rendered my country," but such abuse was heaped upon him—his name was "execrated in the most opprobious terms" whenever he "appeared in the streets of Boston"—that he determined to leave public life. He moved from Boston back to Braintree. Law and politics, he said, "had exhausted my health, brought on a pain in my breast, and complaint in my lungs, which seriously threaten my life, and compelled me to throw off a great part of the load of business, both public and private, and return to my farm in the country." He left for the country with bitter thoughts. "I have stood by the people much longer than they would stand by themselves. But I have learned wisdom by experience; I shall certainly become more retired and cautious; I shall certainly mind my own farm and my own office."

Back in Braintree Adams found the days dragged by. His doctor advised a trip to mineral springs in Connecticut, and although he felt guilty about it Adams agreed to go. "I feel as if I ought not to saunter, and loiter, and trifle away this time; I feel as if I ought to be employed for the benefit of my fellow man in some way or other." But to work for his fellow man meant taking sides, and that Adams could not at the moment do. "I am, for what I can see, quite left alone in the world."

The lethargy lingered through the summer. A trip over the circuit proved "the most flat, insipid, spiritless, tasteless journey that ever I took. . . . I slumber and mope all day." Adams perked up once when, shortly after finishing a plea to the jury, someone told him that people were saying "that Mr. Adams has been making the finest speech I ever heard in my life. He's equal to the greatest orator that ever spoke in Greece or Rome." Ah, said Adams to himself, "what an advantage it is to have the passions, prejudices, and interests of the whole audience in a man's favor."

Adams knew he could win the audience over if he would throw in with the patriots; he knew, too, he could have a variety of honors if he sided with the government. His mind refused to let him join either side. The chance for wealth attracted him immensely, and during these months he referred off and on to the subject in his diary. Rich men, he wrote, "feel the strength and importance which their riches give them in the world; their courage and spirits are buoyed up, their imaginations are inflated by them."

The depth of his depression came in the fall of 1772, as his thirty-seventh birthday approached. He noted dismally that a house in Boston, his farm in Braintree, and three hundred pounds in pocket were "all that the most intense application to study and business has been able to accomplish." The need for money determined Adams to reopen his office in Boston and pick up the remains of his once thriving practice. The return proved rougher than expected. One October morning he stood in a printing office talking with friends when James Otis swept in, "his eyes fishy and fiery." After chatting of other things, this exchange took place:

OTIS: You will never learn military exercise.
ADAMS: Aye, why not?
OTIS: That you have a head for it, needs no commentary, but not a heart.
ADAMS: Aye, how do you know? You never searched my heart.
OTIS: Yes, I have;—tried with one year's service, dancing from Boston to Braintree, and from Braintree to Boston; moping about the streets of this town as hipped as Father Flynt at ninety, and

seemingly regardless of everything but to get money enough to carry smoothly through the world.

After reporting this dialogue, Adams added: "This is the rant of Mr. Otis concerning me, and I suppose of two-thirds of the town."

Two months later, on December 29, 1772, Samuel Adams stopped by with a friend to invite John Adams to give the Boston Massacre Day oration, which, pushed by Samuel Adams to keep the people properly tensed up, had by then become an annual event. John Adams refused. ". . . I should only expose myself to the lash of ignorant and malicious tongues on both sides of the question," he wrote in his diary. "Besides that, I was too old to make declamations."

However, the next night John spent the evening with Samuel Adams. Previously, he had been disturbed by Samuel's hotheadedness, his rantings against the government. This particular evening Samuel seemed different. John found him "more cool, genteel, and agreeable than common; concealed and restrained his passions, etc." The next evening, December 31, uncovered something even more surprising to John Adams. "I found that my constitutional or habitual infirmities have not entirely forsaken me." It had started out as an innocuous evening with old acquaintances, then in the midst of a quiet conversation "I found the old warmth, heat, violence, acrimony, bitterness, sharpness of my temper and expression was not departed. I said there was no more justice left in Britain than there was in hell; that I wished for war, and that the whole Bourbon family was upon the back of Great Britain." All this filled Adams with remorse. "I cannot but reflect upon myself with severity for these rash, inexperienced, boyish, raw, and awkward expressions. A man who has not better government of his tongue, nor more command of his temper, is unfit for everything but children's play and the company of boys."

Having written that, John Adams went to bed. The next afternoon he wrote in his diary: "I have felt very well and been in very good spirits all day. I never was happier in my whole life than I have been since I returned to Boston. I feel easy and composed and contented." Adams went visiting again that evening and found out that his old friends among the patriots still held him in high regard. "Warren thought I was rather a cautious man," Adams reported, "but that he could not say I ever trimmed; when I spoke at all, I always spoke my sentiments. This was a little soothing to my proud heart, no doubt."

New Year's Day 1773 marked John Adams' re-entrance into politics on the side of the patriots. Though doubts arose occasionally, he never abandoned the cause he re-adopted that day.

Once Adams had committed himself, he found it hard to censure any of the patriots' actions. In December 1773 a group of masked men dumped three cargoes of tea in the Boston harbor. "This is the most magnificent movement of all," Adams wrote, forgetting for the moment his antipathy toward mob action or the willful destruction of property. "There is a dignity, a majesty, a sublimity, in this last effort of the patriots, that I greatly admire. The people should never rise without doing something to be remembered, something notable, and striking. This destruction of the tea is so bold, so daring, so firm, intrepid and inflexible, and it must have so important consequences, and so lasting, that I cannot but consider it as an epocha in history."

Enthusiasm for the patriots' cause, however, did not dim Adams' awareness of what England's waywardness had done to his personal fortunes. "I don't receive a shilling a week," he told his wife in May 1774. "We must contrive as many ways as we can to save expenses; for we may have calls to contribute very largely, in proportion to our circumstances, to prevent other very honest people from suffering for want, besides our own loss in point of business and profit."

Adams was now approaching forty, and the fact disheartened him. "My life has been a continual scene of fatigue, vexation, labor and anxiety," he wrote to his wife in June 1774, while on the circuit. "I have four children. I had a pretty estate from my father; I have been assisted by your father; I have done the greatest business in the province; I have had the very richest clients in the province. Yet I am poor, in comparison with others." The fault to some extent was, admittedly, his, the result of an expensive house in Boston and of spending "an estate in books." But much of the blame should fall on England. "These would have been indiscretions, if the impeachment of the judges, the Boston Port Bill, etc., had never happened; but by these unfortunate interruptions of my business from these causes, these indiscretions became almost fatal to me. . . ."

Adams wrote this shortly after he had been told of his election as a delegate to represent Massachusetts in the impending first session of the Continental Congress. He wished, he told his wife, he were off the circuit and settled in his library at home, where "I might be furbishing up my old reading in law and history, that I might appear with less indecency before a variety of gentlemen, whose educations, travels, experience, family, fortune, and everything will give them a vast superiority to me, and I fear even to some of my companions." Meekness was not a pose Adams could hold long, and as he continued his letter he quickly talked himself out of it. "I thank God I have a head and heart, and hands, which, if once fully exerted together, will succeed in the world as well as those of the mean-spirited, low-minded, fawning, obsequious scoundrels who have long hoped that my integrity would be an obstacle in my way, and enable them to outstrip me in the race. . . . I will not willingly see blockheads, whom I have the pleasure to despise, elevated above me and insolently triumphing over me."

Earlier commitments forced Adams to remain away from home and on the circuit the week before he set out for Philadelphia and, filled with loneliness and trepidation, he poured out his thoughts to his wife in a series of letters. The prevalence of sin dominated much of his thought. Vice overruns New England, he said, sounding much like a seventeenth-century divine, and it all springs from "the political innovations of the last ten years." Not only England but the failings of New Englanders themselves were to blame. "There is not a sin which prevails more universally and has prevailed longer than prodigality in furniture, equipage, apparel, and diet. And I believe this vice, this sin, has as large a share in drawing down the judgments of Heaven as any. And perhaps the punishment that is inflicted may work medicinally and cure the disease."

The imminence of mob rule also troubled his thoughts. In early July 1774, a mob had broken into the house of a Falmouth man and terrified his wife and family. Adams, in reporting the incident to his wife, said: "These private mobs I do and will detest. If popular commotions can be justified in opposition to attacks upon the constitution, it can be only when fundamentals are invaded, nor then unless for absolute necessity, and with great caution. But these tarrings and featherings, this breaking open houses by rude and insolent rabble in resentment for private wrongs, or in pursuance of private prejudices and passions must be discountenanced. It cannot be excused even upon any principle which can be entertained by a good citizen, a worthy member of society."

The Tories Adams encountered on the circuit talked of little else but the internal violence that would come to pass if the colonists rebelled. Adams admitted their picture "must be granted to be a likeness," but he saw the choice as the lesser of two evils. "Shall we submit to Parliamentary taxation to avoid mobs? Will not Parliamentary taxation, if established, occasion vices, crimes, and follies infinitely more numerous, dangerous, and fatal to the community? . . . Are insolence, abuse, and impudence more tolerable in a magistrate than in a subject?" He continued:

We seldom ever hear any solid reasoning. . . . I wish always to discuss the question without all painting, pathos, rhetoric, or flourish of every kind. And the question seems to me to be, whether the American colonies are to be considered as a distinct community so far as to have a right to judge for themselves when the fundamentals of their government are destroyed or invaded, or whether they are to be considered as a part of the whole British empire, the whole English nation so far as to be bound in honor, conscience, or by the general sense of the whole nation. However, if this was the rule, I believe it is very far from the general sense of the whole nation, that America should be taxed by the British Parliament. . . . It is very certain that the sense of Parliament is not the sense of the empire, nor a sure indication of it.

It is a fundamental, inherent, and unalienable right of the people, that they have some check, influence, or control in their supreme legislature. If the right of taxation is conceded to Parliament, the Americans have no check or influence at all left.

Adams saw more clearly than most men of his day the way of the future. War between America and Great Britain could not be avoided, and Adams used all his spare time on this final tour of the circuit endeavoring to work out a rationale for revolt. In his travels he met a patriot who had arrived at his position casually, ignorant of "every rope in the ship." This angered Adams, who had reached his decision only after much thought and who, having sided at last with the patriots, even now went "mourning in my heart all the day long."

Adams would act only when he had reasoned through the question, but once he had justified revolt in his mind, it did not follow that he held high hopes for the future. His sense of sin in man was too strong. "Great things are wanted to be done, and little things only I fear can be done," he wrote shortly before setting out for Philadelphia. "I dread the thought of the Congress's falling short of the expectations of the continent, but especially of the people of this province." For all his doubts about mankind, he remained a skeptic, not a cynic. His skepticism never reduced him to empty bitterness or the belief that all action was hopeless. He had hoped things could be improved at least slightly, if approached slowly. He had, in short, the quality of a first-rate intelligence, which has been defined as "the ability to hold two opposed ideas in the mind at the same time, and still retain the ability to function. One should, for example, be able to see that things are hopeless and yet be determined to make them otherwise."

Shortly before he left Falmouth for home, then for Philadelphia, John Adams had a long talk with Jonathan Sewall, his closest friend, who had traveled the circuit with him for the last time. Sewall had committed himself to remain loyal to Great Britain. He urged Adams not to attend Congress. No, he would go *with my friends,* said Adams with emphasis. "I have passed my Rubicon. I will never change. Sink or swim, live or die, survive or perish, I am with my country from this day on."

3

"Be It Resolved. . . ."

On the morning of June 7 after the delegates passed beneath the king's arms decorating the main entrance and into the State House, they turned left and moved between large paneled doors into the handsome chamber on the first floor that the Pennsylvania Assembly had loaned them for their meetings. The room was lined on two sides by long windows that admitted plenty of light even on overcast days. During Philadelphia's humid summers the windows were cracked to let in a breeze, but when tempers broke and voices rose someone might suggest they be closed to prevent passers-by from hearing what went on within. The occasional fury of the debate could shock newcomers. One newly arrived member who had venerated Congress and most of the delegates was astonished, once inside the room, to see "how little of the spirit of [the Declaration of Independence] actuated many of the members of Congress who had just before subscribed it." One day he heard Samuel Chase of Maryland insinuate from the floor that New England troops had caused the failure of the Canadian invasion. The failure, John Adams ripped back, emanated solely from "the impudence of the gentleman from Maryland," and if Chase could only see his failings, he would beg from his knees for Congress's forgiveness, then "afterwards retire with shame and spend the remainder of his life in sackcloth and ashes, deploring the mischief he has done his country."

Toward the far end of the room at a small table sat Charles Thomson, permanent secretary of Congress, and nearby at another table President John Hancock, his back to twin fireplaces along the east wall. Hancock's presence at that table gave Samuel Adams a twinge every time he entered the room.

John Hancock
AGE: 40   MERCHANT

No man enjoyed the pleasures wealth could give him more than John Hancock and, through it, he could give others. He rolled through life in a glorious array of colors, favoring lavender suits and bright yellow coaches, among other hues in the spectrum. "His apparel was sumptuously embroidered with gold and silver and lace and all the other decorations fashionable amongst men of fortune of that day," an acquaintance recalled. "He rode, especially upon public occasions, with six beautiful bays, and with servants in livery. He was graceful and prepossessing in manners, and very passionately addicted to what are called the elegant pleasures of life, to dancing, music, concerts, routs, assemblies, card parties, rich wines, social dinners and festivities." He relished what Jefferson called the "tinsel of life" but with such open satisfaction that few men resented the display.

Men who fell out over politics could at least agree on one thing—John Hancock had large failings mixed with modest virtues:

A BOSTON TORY: His understanding was of the dwarf size, but his ambition . . . was upon the gigantic. He was free from immoralities, and objects of charity often felt the effect of his riches. His mind was a mere *tabula rasa,* and had he met with a good artist he would have enstamped upon it such character as would have made him a most useful member of society.

A BOSTON WHIG: Your old friend figures away in the usual style. Sometimes the pendulum swings one way, and sometimes the other—I mean with regard to Whiggism and Toryism—but never fails to swing uniformly against all that won't bow down and worship a very silly image.

A COLLEAGUE IN CONGRESS: He was fond of the ceremonies of public life, but wanted industry and punctuality in business. His conversation was desultory, and his manners much influenced by frequent attacks of the gout, which gave a hypercritical peevishness to his temper. With all these infirmities he was a disinterested patriot, and made large sacrifices of an ample estate to the liberties and independence of his country.

John Adams, who rarely wavered when judging others, found it hard to take a consistent line on Hancock. One moment he called him "a leaky vessel" who betrayed state secrets, the next he was "our amiable friend Hancock." Once he railed at "the sordid meanness" of Hancock's soul hidden beneath "the most splendid affection of generosity, liberality, and patriotism," only to be suddenly staggered by the man's openhandedness. "On a visit to Mrs. Yard's this evening I was informed by her that your lady and children proposed to go into Boston with an intention of taking the smallpox by inoculation," Hancock said in a note dropped at Adams' boarding house, "and as the season is warm, and the present process of treating that disorder requires all the air that can possibly be had, and as my situation in Boston is as much blessed with a free air as most others, I made a tender of my house and garden for their use. . . . The fruit in the garden shall be at their control, and a maid servant and the others in the house shall afford them every convenience that appertains to the house."

As the son of a clergyman "whose circumstances in life were not above mediocrity," Hancock had lucked into his life of luxury. The father died when Hancock was nine. His mother soon after married another clergyman of mediocre circumstances. She took Hancock's brother and sister with her, but a rich uncle, Thomas Hancock, carried John into his sumptuous house on Beacon Hill, where his childless wife Lydia made him "the object of her fondest affection on this side of heaven." Uncle Thomas sent him to Boston Latin, to Harvard College, then, as a clerk, drew him into his lucrative mercantile business. When twenty-three he went to London to meet the firm's agents, and while there he saw the funeral of George II and the coronation of George III. He returned to Boston with his mind packed with memories of the way the rich lived abroad, but he repressed a yearning for the high life relished in London. Instead, he "became an example to all the young men of the town," said an incredulous friend. "Wholly devoted to business, he was regular and punctual at his store as the sun in his course."

Three years after his return Uncle Thomas died, and at the age of twenty-seven Hancock took control "of what was reputed to be the greatest fortune ever amassed in New England," a biographer has said. "It was fortunate that the business was substantial, for he lacked his uncle's acumen, and he was taking the helm in very difficult times." Parliament had recently passed a revenue act that forecast the end of the old "live and let live" policy toward the colonies. Customs collections were to be tightened up, smuggling attacked more vigorously. Then, in 1765, came news of the Stamp Act. Every bill of lading that passed through Hancock's firm, every legal document it filed in court, every advertisement for goods it took in the press would hereafter be taxed with stamps that had to be purchased through royal agents.

At first Hancock accepted the tax as a necessary evil. "Our trade is prodigiously embarrassed, and must shortly be ruined under the present circumstances," he said, "but we must submit." A few weeks later his opinion changed. He now believed "an opposition to the Stamp Act is highly commendable." Soon he thought Americans were "a gone people" if they accepted the act; then he was convinced they would "never suffer themselves to be made slaves of by a submission to that d____d act."

The swing in sentiment owed much to Samuel Adams. It was remarked that Hancock was "as closely attached to the hindermost part of Mr. *Adams* as the rattles are affixed to the tail of a rattlesnake." Before Hancock knew how it had happened he, who had said early in the agitation that "I seldom meddle with politics," found himself in the provincial legislature. "This town has done a wise thing today," Adams said after the election. "They have made that young man's fortune their own." Adams manipulated his election to the council, then later as speaker *pro tem* of the legislature. Both times the governor vetoed the appointments, refusing to work with a declared enemy of the government.

It was an open secret Hancock was the colony's, if not the continent's, greatest smuggler. (He had learned the craft from an expert, Uncle Thomas, who owed his fortune, it was said, to "his importing from St. Eustatius great quantities of tea in molasses hogsheads, which sold at a very great advance.") When one of his ships, the *Liberty,* arrived loaded with contraband wine, the crew locked up a curious customs officer, landed the cargo unmolested, and sent it on the way to customers. When the government sued for treble the value of the wine, he hired John Adams to fight the case. But when a few months later the British eased the pinch on his pocketbook nerve, he stepped back to reassess the situation. He now saw that Samuel Adams went "further than appeared to him warrantable." He suggested the town meeting might investigate "the great deficiency" occasioned by Samuel Adams' tenure as tax collector. Governor Thomas Hutchinson rejoiced to hear Hancock had stopped going to Adams' political club and "seems to have a new set of acquaintance." He approved Hancock's election as speaker of the house.

Yet within a year he had been enticed back to Adams' fold. The tax on tea imposed by Parliament did not bother him so much as the fact that the subsidized East India Company would soon be unloading tea on the American market at cut-rate prices, cheaper than the smuggled Dutch tea people had been drinking. Hancock, it happened, had a warehouse full of the Dutch tea leaves. He now rejoined Samuel Adams' crusade for American freedom. As speaker, he approved publication of several of Hutchinson's letters, stolen by Benjamin Franklin in London, which supposedly showed the governor working "to overthrow the government and to introduce arbitrary power into the province." He rejoined the committee of correspondence he had once abandoned. He helped organize the meeting that led to the dumping of the tea from London in Boston harbor. A few months later he delivered the annual oration Adams had devised to keep the Boston Massacre fresh in the people's memory. "Let every parent tell the shameful story to his listening children till tears of pity glisten in their eyes, and boiling passions shake their tender frames," he said in his ghost-written speech.

When a group of drunken British soldiers attacked his mansion on Beacon Hill he carried Aunt Lydia and Dorothy Quincy, whom he had been courting in a desultory way for four years, out to Lexington. Soon after he heard the British were on their way to Lexington; he prepared to join the militia on the village green but Samuel Adams convinced him the cause could not afford to lose him in a skirmish. The two men went into hiding. Five days later they were on their way to Philadelphia for the opening of the Second Continental Congress.

Two weeks after it convened the Congress chose Hancock as its president. Benjamin Harrison, who could abide few Northerners, helped engineer the election. He had found Hancock a convivial companion who, shorn of his Boston accent, might pass for a gentleman. Hancock quickly proved to have been a superb choice. His benign presence helped alleviate Southern distaste for New England. He moderated the often bitter debates with skill. "Mr. Hancock had those talents which were calculated to make him appear to more advantage as chairman, than in the debates of a public body," a contemporary not especially fond of him remarked. "He discovered a fine address, a great impartiality, sufficient spirit to command attention, and preserve order. His voice and manner were much in his favor, and his experience, in public business, gave him ease and dignity."

But Hancock wished to be more than president of Congress. He wanted to be commander in chief of the continental army. When John Adams rose to propose a candidate for the post, Hancock listened "with visible pleasure; but when I came to describe Washington for the commander, I never remarked a more sudden and striking change of countenance. Mortification and resentment were expressed as forcibly as his face could exhibit them. Mr. Samuel Adams seconded the action, and that did not soften the President's physiognomy."

Hancock resigned himself to the decision—later he named a son after Washington—and settled down to running Congress with good humor and tact. Sometimes he let matters slide that called for prompt attention, but colleagues excused the fault. "The great and important business in which he is constantly employed and the almost immense number of letters which he is constantly receiving on the most interesting subjects makes it impossible for him to attend to them all and lesser matters must be neglected," a delegate explained to a friend who wondered why Hancock ignored his letters. Once he shocked the brethren from New England by proposing "that Madeira wine may be imported" despite a previous agreement against such action. "He meant to please the Southern delegates who insist on having wine," it was said—self-interest, too, may have been involved— and if so the ploy worked. "I do not know what to think of these men" from New England, Harrison told Washington. "They seem exceeding hearty in the cause but still wish to keep everything among themselves. Our President is quite a different cast —noble, disinterested, and generous to a very great degree."

To escape the heat of Philadelphia, Congress in 1775 took off the month of August. The holiday ended with news of one "of the most unlikely things within the whole compass of possibility" —John Hancock had married Dorothy Quincy. He brought his "agreeable lady" back to Philadelphia, and she "honors us with her presence and contributes much to our good humor as well as to the happiness of the President," so much so that the day the delegates gathered for their first session, "Mr. Hancock having a touch of gout, there was no President in the chair."

After the holiday those who favored independence began to campaign relentlessly for their cause. Not once during the next ten months did they relax the pressure. Hancock stayed above the battle, though it was rumored that he favored those for reconciliation with Britain. He supposedly "courted" James Duane of New York and John Dickinson of Pennsylvania, then the leaders of the anti-independence faction, "and leaned so partially in their favor, that Mr. Samuel Adams had become very bitter against Mr. Hancock, and spoke of him with great asperity in private circles." Still, during the great debates in June and early July 1776 Hancock could, with his now good friend Harrison serving as chairman of the committee of the whole, have spoken from the floor against independence if he had wished. Apparently he did not, otherwise John Adams would have passed the word to posterity.

Shortly after the bell in the State House tower rang the hour of ten on June 7 Hancock rapped the delegates to order. Although they were on the whole hard-working, punctuality did not number among their virtues. As a rule they straggled in through the morning, many of them delayed by committee meetings often held before Congress convened. On days when important matters were to be debated, Hancock had to plead for "the delegates to be upon honor to meet punctually at ten o'clock." This morning he saw at once he had a quorum present and nodded to Andrew McNair, the doorkeeper, who swung shut the doors, took up his post outside, and was ready to bar all but tardy delegates from joining the secret discussion within.

In life the trivial often adulterates the momentous. This day that Samuel Adams thought the most important question "ever agitated in America would be decided" opened on a minor note. The delegates began by pondering the problem of a ship that had been commandeered by the commodore of the continental fleet. They resolved that the owner should be paid for his loss. Next, they discussed the quality of "powder manufactured at Mr. O. Eve's mill." These matters settled, Richard Henry Lee of Virginia, as the senior member of his delegation, rose to introduce his resolution.

Richard Henry Lee

AGE: 44 POLITICIAN

There were six brothers—Philip Ludwell, Thomas Ludwell, Richard Henry, Francis Lightfoot, William, and Arthur. The elder two became lawyers, Francis was satisfied to be a country gentleman, William settled in London as a merchant, and Arthur dabbled in medicine, then turned to law. The Lees of Virginia had been in politics for a century, and while none of the brothers abandoned family tradition, Richard alone tried to make the avocation into a career. He took pride in his plantation, Chantilly, particularly the peach brandy produced there; he lived off the sometimes meager income from his tobacco crop, but he lived for politics.

Tutors taught him at home; then, like all the brothers but Francis, he went to England for further education. His father had died before Lee returned home. He settled at Chantilly. He married. He became colonel of the Westmoreland County militia, and in 1755 offered his company to General Braddock for the march on Fort Dusquesne. Braddock rejected the offer, but Lee did not give up hope for military glory until a hunting accident left him with a maimed hand. (Though he had not the slightest chance of seeing active duty, delegates in Congress always addressed him as "colonel.") He moved into public life by the usual route for Southern gentlemen—first as a justice of the peace, then as a member of the House of Burgesses. There were four Lees in the legislature—Philip sat on the council, Thomas, Richard, and Francis in the house. Thomas "was the delight of the eyes of Virginia and by far the most popular man they had," according to George Wythe. "But Richard was not."

Richard brought a crusading spirit into a house packed with easy-going gentlemen. His standards were high and severe. (And they remained so. "It would have been better," he said after the Revolution when he heard Virginians refused to pay debts owed to British merchants, "to have remained the honest slaves of Britain than become dishonest freemen.") In an early speech that won little applause, he called for a check on the spread of slavery. Twice he demanded an investigation of John Robinson's management of the provincial treasury. Robinson, an old foe of Lee's father, doubled as speaker of the house and treasurer. He used his power adroitly to frustrate young Lee's curiosity until it was swallowed up by a greater cause—the Stamp Act. Stamp duties, Lee said, violated "the essential principles of the British constitution." Such unlawful "taxation without consent," he warned, may produce in Americans "a fatal resentment of parental care being converted into tyrannical usurpation." But a few months after this speech the supposedly affronted Lee did an odd thing: he applied for the job of stamp agent for Virginia. A short while later he withdrew the application—probably someone in the family convinced him it would be political suicide even to consider the job—and set about denouncing the Stamp Act with a vigor and invective equaled only by Samuel Adams. That opprobrious act, he now said, converted a once kindly mother country into "an arbitrary, cruel, and oppressive step-dame"; the agents chosen to enforce it were an "infernal crew of hireling miscreants"; George III had transformed himself into a "tyrant" and his servants into "foes of mankind," "devils of despotism." Lee led the opposition in the House of Burgesses, with George Wythe and Patrick Henry as allies, and back in Westmoreland County, months before anyone else in America, he organized the first boycott of British goods.

Public revelation of his application for stamp agent almost ruined his career when it leaked out in 1766. Its effect was blunted by the death that year of Robinson, who, it turned out, had indeed misused his power as treasurer to make some £100,000 in unauthorized loans to friends among the old guard. Ten years later when John Adams wondered about the "jealousies and divisions" in the Virginia delegation in Congress, Wythe put the blame on Richard Henry Lee. This puzzled Adams even more, for Lee seemed to be "a scholar, a gentleman, a man of uncommon eloquence, and an agreeable man." All true, said Wythe, but the old guard, among whom Benjamin Harrison counted, had never forgiven Lee for provoking an investigation into Robinson's affairs. "This made him so many enemies that he never had recovered his reputation, but was still heartily hated by great numbers."

The Robinson affair slipped into the background when news arrived in 1767 of the Townshend duties imposed by Parliament. They were, of course, "arbitrary, unjust, and destructive," but more than that they made the fight for Lee what it had long been for Samuel Adams—one between the wicked and the just, between the corrupt and the virtuous. "It is some comfort to have the virtuous on our side," he now said. Americans, "from one end of the continent to the other," he wrote with that boundless optimism of a righteous man engaged in a great cause, "appear too wise, too brave, and much too honest, to be either talked, terrified, or bribed from the assertion of just, equitable, and long possessed rights." He buttressed this optimism with some practical politics. Upon the foundation of "virtuous principles" that already united the colonies some sort of continental political organization must be built, and with that end in view Lee in 1773 began corresponding with Samuel Adams in Boston and John Dickinson in Philadelphia. From the exchange of letters came the creation of a chain of committees of correspondence designed to spread the "true state of affairs" from one end of the continent to the other.

Lee's letters to Adams show him to be no less skillful a politician than the "old deluder" himself. "Should any material information concerning the American cause reach Boston," he wrote when the House of Burgesses was about to convene, "I should be glad to have particular intelligence from you. At the same time, it will be highly conducive to the general good that your corresponding committee write a public letter to ours on any such occasion. Its reception whilst the assembly is sitting will be the most fit time for information coming to hand." With help from a new young member, Thomas Jefferson, Lee got the house to order a day of "fasting, humiliation, and prayer" throughout Virginia to mark the day Boston would be closed by the Port Act; to condemn that act as a "most violent and dangerous attempt to destroy the constitutional liberty and rights of all British America"; and to issue a call for a meeting of delegates from all the colonies to discuss their grievances with the mother country.

At the First Congress the acquaintance made with Samuel Adams through letters ripened into friendship. As political partners they complemented each other perfectly. Adams stayed "active in preparing and doing business out of doors," while Lee served as floor manager for the cause. Lee had the presence for public performance: he was a tall man, over six feet, with pale skin set off by a thatch of sandy red hair, and he spoke easily in a soothing, "harmonious voice, occasionally punctuating his speeches with the mangled hand he now carried swathed in a black kerchief." In the First Congress he and Patrick Henry "took at once the lead in that assembly and by the high style of their eloquence, were, in the first days of the session, looked up to as *primi inter pares.*" The delegates rejected his address to the people of England—Lee did not excel as a writer, and Congress rarely thereafter called upon him to draw up public statements—but otherwise he judged the First Congress a complete success. The nonimportation agreement accepted by the delegates displayed a unity among the colonies he thought would surely force the mother country to back down. (So certain, indeed, was Lee of peace that a year earlier he had sent two of his children to be educated in England, where, during the Revolution, their classmates taunted them with the hope that "their father's head might soon be seen set on a pike on Tower Hill.")

Lee came to the Second Congress as determined as Samuel

Adams for independence. They sounded so much alike in their letters that even friends would have found it hard to tell who had written what. "The measure of the British crimes is running over," went one of Lee's Adams-like sentences in 1776, "and the barbarous spoilation of the East is crying to heaven for vengeance against the destroyers of the human race." By April it had become clear Congress would continue to dodge the question of independence until some colony, through instructions to its delegation, forced it to be discussed, or, as Francis Lightfoot Lee put it, "till the people bring it before them."

Richard Henry Lee devised a strategy to end the stalemate. "Virginia has hitherto taken the lead in great affairs, and many now look to her with anxious expectation, hoping that the spirit, wisdom, and energy of her councils will rouse America," he wrote Patrick Henry in the late spring of 1776. Soon after the letter arrived the Virginia convention voted to order its delegation in Congress to introduce a resolution calling for independence. The measure passed May 15. Thomas Nelson carried it to Philadelphia and turned it over to Lee, the senior member of the Virginia delegation, to present to Congress.

"Be it resolved," Lee said in his harmonious voice on June 7,

That these United Colonies are, and of right ought to be, free and independent States, that they are absolved from all allegiance to the British Crown, and that all political connection between them and the State of Great Britain is, and ought to be, totally dissolved.

That it is expedient forthwith to take the most effectual measures for forming foreign alliances.

That a plan of confederation be prepared and transmitted to the respective Colonies for their consideration and approbation.

Lee's words carried Congress toward treasonable ground. The secretary in the official journal ignored all that Lee had said and noted only that "certain resolutions" had been "moved and discussed."

4

The Great Debate

Standard procedure required discussion of important measures to be postponed a day after first being placed before Congress. This gave the delegates a chance to ponder the matter and clarify their views. There was some discussion on June 7, but it was eventually cut short by a resolution calling for Lee's proposals to "be referred till tomorrow; and, that the members be enjoined to attend punctually at 10 o'clock in order to take them into consideration."

The next morning Congress assembled on time and at once resolved itself into a committee of the whole. This allowed the discussion to proceed with easy informality and without the secretary keeping an official record of what was said. John Hancock stepped away from the chair, and Benjamin Harrison of Virginia took over as presiding officer.

$\mathcal{B}$enjamin $\mathcal{H}$arrison

The story goes that when Congress chose Hancock as President he "hesitated, or pretended to hesitate, to take the seat to which he had been elected." The imposing Benjamin Harrison of Virginia stepped in and covered the awkward situation with "ready good humor." He threw his arms around Hancock and lifted him into the presidential chair, then turned to the room and said in a loud voice:

"We will show mother Britain how little we care for her, by making a Massachusetts man our President, whom she has excluded from pardon by a public proclamation."

Harrison no more fit the stereotype of the sedate, cultivated Southern planter than his friend Hancock did that of the puritanical New Englander. He exuded the arrogance, self-confidence, and authority of an aristocrat but looked and sounded like a bawdy, red-faced farmer. In his youth he had been "very muscular" but now the muscles sagged and he had ballooned into a fat man. "This rose from his mode of living, which was highly convivial," a contemporary explained; "he enjoyed and indulged in the pleasure of the table, though never beyond the limits of propriety. This habit, however, tended much to impair the vigor of his constitution; and his features, which in early life were handsome, became at last coarse." In later years when Harrison had cut back on his drinking he insisted old age had not slowed him down, but only the error in earlier days of "having pursued the foolish fashions of the time, and abandoned good old Madeira for light French wines."

The New Englanders in Congress disliked him. He is "an uncommonly large man, and appears rather rough in his address and speech," one of them reported home. Another remembered him with rancor decades after they had ceased to meet. "Harrison was another Sir John Falstaff, excepting his larcenies and robberies, his conversation disgusting to every man of delicacy or decorum, profane, perpetually ridiculing the Bible, calling it the worst book in the world." Samuel Adams and Harrison tangled early and often. Once Adams forced the cancellation of a ball which the wives of General Washington and John Hancock had planned to attend; he held it wrong for the land's leading ladies to dance when the nation fasted and prayed for victory. "Spent some time pleasantly," a visitor to Adams' lodgings reported the night the ball was canceled, "until Col. Harrison came to rebuke Samuel Adams for using his influence for the stopping of this entertainment, which he declared was legal, just and laudable. Many arguments were used by all present to convince him of the impropriety at this time but all to no effect; so, as he came out of humor, he so returned to appearance."

Little in Harrison's background prepared him for the moral uplift of a Samuel Adams. He received a relaxed education at William and Mary College, married young, and entered the House of Burgesses when only twenty-three. He got along well with his colleagues in the House, except for Richard Henry Lee, whose humorless approach to politics depressed him. Once in Philadelphia Harrison and Lee showed up for a late supper "very high." It was not their drinking that called for remark but their drinking together; the two men detested one another. Harrison did his best to get Lee dropped from the Virginia delegation in Congress. He started a whispering campaign that accused Lee of ordering "his overseer to demand produce or bullion for rent" from his tenants instead of accepting pay in the depreciated continental dollars, "but this was proved to be false by the fullest declaration of the overseer" and "to the double mortification of said H____" Lee was re-elected to his seat.

Harrison attended the First Congress and there said "he would have come on foot rather than not come," an extraordinary remark from that "indolent, luxurious" gentleman. Back in Philadelphia in 1775 for the Second Congress, he circulated mainly among the opulent and conservative delegates—Thomas Willing and Robert Morris of Pennsylvania, James Duane of New York,

The Great Debate 39

and, of course, John Hancock of Massachusetts. He lived handsomely in a large house on the edge of town, so handsomely indeed, said a genteel acquaintance, that he "exceeded, in some degree, the limits of prudence," and had to borrow heavily from his friend Willing. "This loan at one time amounted to so large a sum" that it took Harrison years to pay it off in painfully small installments. When the British forged a paragraph from an intercepted letter of Harrison's wherein he appeared to be philandering with "little Kate the washerwoman's daughter over the way, trim and rosy as the morning," no one, particularly among the New England delegates, doubted the lines were true.

The New Englanders had practical as well as moral reasons to dislike Harrison. Beneath the layers of fat and the convivial personality lay one of the ablest political minds in the colonies. Even an enemy agreed "he was well acquainted with the forms of public business." Only Roger Sherman and Samuel Adams equaled him as a manipulator. Washington depended on him for advice and to protect the army's interests in Congress. Harrison spoke rarely from the floor but was listened to when he did. The delegates consistently placed him on important committees, and because he was so "often nominated with [me] in business," the adroit John Adams said, "I took no notice of his vices or follies, but treated him, and Mr. Hancock, too, with uniform politeness."

Harrison had "strong state interests" and fought remorselessly to protect Virginia's rights and powers, but enemies admitted he seldom lost sight of what was good for the United Colonies. On March 5, 1776, he was chosen to be permanent chairman whenever Congress resolved itself into a committee of the whole house, an informal arrangement that allowed the delegates to discuss issues and vote upon them off the record. Together the team of Hancock and Harrison carried Congress through the tedious days of debate that led up to independence. Fittingly, he is remembered for cracking a joke the day Congress signed the Declaration.

As the great debate got under way on June 8 the essence of the issue—of all great political issues in a democracy, for that matter—appeared almost at once. Those who resisted independence said America should defer "to take any capital step till the voice of the people drove us into it." The people, these men said, "were our power, and without them our declaration could not be carried into effect." Those for independence answered, "the people wait for us to lead the way." Furthermore, *"they* are in favor of the measure, tho' the instructions given by some of their *representatives* are not."

Much of the debate centered on the Middle Colonies, where the people, said one man, "were not yet ripe for bidding adieu to the British connection but," he added, "were fast ripening and in a short time would join in the general voice of America."

During the afternoon the Pennsylvania Assembly sent down from its second-floor chamber in the State House a new set of instructions for its delegation. The assembly did not encourage its delegates to vote for independence, but it now no longer forbade them to do so. James Wilson rose to speak on the revised instructions.

James Wilson
AGE: 33   LAWYER

He stood over six feet tall, so erect he appeared to be "stooping backward." All agreed that "his features could not be called handsome," that "his manner was a little constrained," that his extreme nearsightedness—he wore thick glasses—gave "the appearance of sternness." Most of the delegates agreed, too, with the colleague who said Wilson "produced greater orations than any other man I have heard," in spite of the broad Scotch accent that sometimes made it hard to catch his words. "His mind, while he spoke, was one blaze of light. Not a word fell from his lips out of time, or out of place, nor could a word be taken from or added to his speeches without injuring."

The words "constituents" and "people" cropped up often in his speeches, sometimes as a ploy to win a point but more often because he believed the public should be consulted on matters that concerned its vital interests. Once, while Congress in secrecy debated a major issue, he moved that the doors of the State House chamber be thrown open, "galleries erected, or an adjournment made to some public building where the people might be accommodated." Yet Wilson was not a man of the people nor did he court their affection. He preferred books to men. If company were to be forced upon him, let it be that of the well-to-do and successful. His conversation with intellectual inferiors was "rare, distant, and reserved." Those who heard him in the courtroom found his manner "rather imposing than persuasive," tinged with arrogance. "His habitual effort seemed to be to subdue without conciliating, and the impression left was more like that of submission to a stern than a humane conqueror." Stern he was, as might be expected of a Scotsman reared in a strict Presbyterian household and trained for the church. Arrogant, too. Yet Wilson was prisoner to an idea—the people were sovereign and all political power originated with them—that shaped his public decisions and sometimes forced him against his nature down a road he had not planned to travel, like the one that led toward independence.

Wilson's parents had promised him to the kirk at birth and sent him to the University of St. Andrews when he was fifteen. He was in the last year of divinity school when his father died, an event Wilson used to escape from his calling by saying he must help support the family. He tried tutoring for a while, then went to Edinburgh to study bookkeeping. "You will perhaps recollect that during your stay here," his teacher wrote years later, "I one day pressed and prevailed with you to take a game at golf at Bruntfield links, a diversion you was totally unfamiliar with. My purpose was to instruct you in it, but how sadly was I mortified at your beating me every round. This, I thought often since, had something prophetic in it. So may it always happen to you and your opponents in all your laudable undertakings."

Feeling cramped and full of an ambition too large for Scotland to accommodate, Wilson came to America in 1765. A job at the College of Philadelphia as a Latin tutor provided enough money to pay for the privilege of reading law in the office of the town's leading lawyer, John Dickinson. While there Dickinson published his famous attack on the Townshend duties, *Letters from a Farmer in Pennsylvania,* which contested Parliament's authority to lay taxes of any kind upon the colonies but conceded its rights to regulate trade. Wilson became curious about the historical basis of this "power of Parliament over us." Research convinced him Parliament in no instance had any authority to legislate for the colonies and this finding led to another even more heretical: *"all the different members of the British empire are* DISTINCT STATES, INDEPENDENT OF EACH OTHER, BUT CON-NECTED TOGETHER UNDER THE SAME SOVER-EIGN." Wilson embodied his ideas in an essay entitled "Consid-erations on the Nature and Extent of the Legislative Authority of the British Parliament." He was a young man on the make, eager for fame, position, and power; to have published such no-tions in 1767 would have branded him as an irremediable radical. He filed the essay away.

After admission to the bar he left the competitive circle of Philadelphia lawyers to build a practice in the village of Reading. Friends in Philadelphia helped when they could—someone di-rected Franklin's wife to him when she wanted a debt in the back country collected—but Reading was a Pennsylvania Dutch town with little affection for a Scotch accent. Wilson moved on, west-ward to Carlisle, and there among the contentious Scotch–Irish his business flourished. Soon he was handling nearly half the cases in the local courthouse, practicing in seven other counties, in Philadelphia, and occasionally in New Jersey and New York. He married, bought a slave, moved into a spacious house. He had a substantial income but wanted a fortune, and in 1773 symptoms appeared of the disease that eventually would bring him down; he began borrowing money to speculate in land. The onset of the Revolution only arrested the disorder.

Wilson published his essay on Parliament's lack of legitimate power over the colonies while the First Congress met in Philadelphia. One of its paragraphs especially impressed the delegates. "All men are by nature, equal and free," Wilson said. "No one has a right to any authority over another without his consent. All lawful government is founded on the consent of those who are subject to it. Such consent was given with a view to insure and to increase the happiness of the governed above what they could enjoy in an independent and unconnected state of nature. The consequence is, that the happiness of the society is the *first* law of every government."

Admiration for his ability earned by the essay carried Wilson into the Second Congress. There, in spite of his bold view on imperial relations, he opposed independence. "We disavow the intention," he said. "We declare that what we aim at, and what we are entrusted by [the people] to pursue, *is the defense and the re-establishment of the constitutional rights of the colonies.*" But let the crown and Parliament beware. "Though an independent empire is not our *wish*, it may—let our oppressors attend—it may be the fate of our countrymen and ourselves," he went on. "Let those who drive us to it answer to their king and to their country for the consequences. We are *desirous* to continue subjects, but we are *determined* to continue *freemen.*"

When Congress learned that the king had hired foreign mercenaries to crush the American rebellion and that a fleet with an army aboard would soon sail for the colonies, Wilson saw that Britain's determination to push on with the war made the decision for separation inevitable. The timing alone remained a matter of debate for him. On June 8, after receiving the Assembly's revised instructions, he said he would vote for independence but that he "still wished a determination on it to be postponed a short time" to let the people of Pennsylvania express their thoughts on the issue and also to give "the constituents of several colonies an opportunity of removing their respective instructions whereby unanimity would probably be obtained."

As the hours slipped past, the nub of the debate revolved around the unity of the colonies. Opponents of an immediate declaration fell back repeatedly on this point. Division among the colonies would not only destroy hope of victory, it would weaken any chance for a foreign alliance, one delegate remarked. "Let us wait," said another, for we may in a few days "receive certain information of the disposition of the French court, from the agent whom we had sent to Paris for that purpose. . . . If this disposition should be favorable, by waiting the event of the present campaign, which we all hoped would be successful, we should have reason to expect an alliance on better terms."

One speaker held that with or without a declaration America's chance for a foreign alliance appeared slim. "France and Spain," he said, "had reason to be jealous of that rising power which would one day certainly strip them of all their American possessions," and so would never help the colonies win their freedom. Others thought that France and Spain's current fear of powerful England would prove stronger than a fear of a potentially threatening America, but even if they should refuse to help "we shall be but where we are; whereas without trying we shall never know whether they will aid us or not."

The usual three o'clock adjournment time came and went. Possibly some of the delegates stepped across Chestnut Street to the tavern for refreshment and others stretched their legs in the State House yard, but the debate rolled on without interruption. Afternoon merged into early evening and still it continued. It became obvious as the discussion meandered on that the opponents to independence were not essentially arguing against independence itself—regardless of their personal views on the matter, most saw the event as inevitable—but to delay a declaration of it long enough to hear what the peace commissioners, rumored to be on their way, had to say. Some wished a foreign alliance to be made before leaping into the dark, others believed the colonies must confederate before they separated. No one in his argument resorted to high-sounding principles or talked about the natural rights of mankind to justify his position. These were practical politicians debating a great issue with practical arguments.

It became apparent as the evening wore on that no decision would be reached that day. Finally, it was resolved "to sit again on Monday next." During the intervening Sunday, the delegates "out of doors might be able to approach some agreement among themselves." Edward Rutledge of South Carolina, who had argued mightily against independence through the long debate, told a friend that night that on Monday he meant to move that the question "should be postponed for three weeks or months." He added, with little enthusiasm, "in the meantime the plan of confederation and the scheme of treaty may go on. I don't know whether I shall succeed in this motion; I think not, it is at least doubtful. However, I must do what is right in my own eyes, and consequences must take care of themselves."

Edward Rutledge
AGE: 26   LAWYER

He looked older than his years. He had a florid face, was nearly bald, and, as someone delicately put it, was "inclining toward corpulency." Yet the delegates called him young Rutledge, not because of his youth but because he had come to the First Congress with his elder brother John. He had not made a good impression at that gathering. "A little unsteady and injudicious," said one delegate. "He has the most indistinct, inarticulate way of speaking."

By June 1776 young Rutledge, out from under his brother's shadow, had steadied enough to lead the band of hard-core reconciliationists with authority and become one of the four or five most influential members of Congress. John Adams, perhaps piqued with his effective opposition to independence, still regarded him as "excessively variable and unsteady" and when he spoke with unaccustomed eloquence and sagacity suspected "he had been instructed out-of-doors by some of the most knowing merchants and statesmen in Philadelphia." Not only what Rutledge said but the way he said it offended Adams. "He shrugs his shoulders, distorts his body, nods and wriggles his head, and looks about with his eyes, from side to side, and speaks thro' his nose, as the Yankees sing." It would have offended Adams even more to know that these gyrations were meant in part to distract listeners from the nonsense Rutledge sometimes retailed. He told a friend "he had been more than once in the awkward predicament of being oppressed with his own incoherence," but convinced that the slow witted in the audience would not "perceive what was sense or the reverse" and that the generous part would indulge him, "made it a positive rule never to sit down, or to hesitate or halt, but to talk on and brave it out with the best countenance he could assume."

John Rutledge, senior by ten years, had watched over Edward as if he were his father, bringing him into his law office as a clerk, then subsidizing a four-year stay in England, where he read law in the Middle Temple. Edward returned home a touch pontifical, prone to pronouncements such as "young gentlemen ought to travel early, because that freedom and ease of behavior which is so necessary cannot be acquired but in early life." He wed the daughter of Henry Middleton; she brought a fortune of £70,000 with her into the marriage. As the last of seven children of a Charleston physician, Edward had been accustomed to a modest way of life; overnight the youngest son became the wealthiest. He purchased land across the street from the houses of his brothers John and Hugh and built a home larger than theirs combined.

Edward's public life began with the First Congress, which he attended with brother John and his father-in-law, both seasoned politicians who probably arranged his election to the delegation. Although Henry Middleton and John spoke for the colony in Congress, they did not intimidate Edward into either silence or modesty. "You may thank your stars you sent prudent men," he wrote home as Congress was disbanding, "and I trust that the youngest is not the least so."

John Rutledge continued to overshadow his brother in the Second Congress until late in 1775, when he returned to South Carolina. From then on few days passed in Congress without some word from E. Rutledge, as an exasperated Northerner noted in his diary: "this occasioned a motion from E. Rutledge" (January 26). . . . "E. Rutledge reported" (February 2). . . . "E. Rutledge vehemently for it" (February 16). . . . "A motion by E. Rutledge" (February 27). . . . "E. Rutledge renewed his motion" (February 28). . . . "A motion by E. Rutledge" (March 6). . . . "E. Rutledge reported" (March 8). . . . "E. Rutledge. . . . was appointed" (March 11). . . . "E. Rutledge was against" (March 13). And so it went. The accolade came in June 1776 when Congress chose E. Rutledge to sit on one of its most important committees, the newly created board of war and ordnance.

Rutledge fought a skillful delaying action against independence, partly with reasonable arguments—it was ridiculous to separate until the colonies had joined in a confederation, and until they were united no foreign power would deign to offer aid—and partly by playing on the fear that the phalanx of New England colonies would dominate the new nation. "I dread their low cunning," he said, "and those levelling principles which men without character and without fortune in general possess, which are so captivating to the lower class of mankind, and which will occasion such a fluctuation of property as to introduce the greatest disorder."

Congress came to order at the usual hour of ten o'clock on Monday morning. An awaiting pile of letters that could no longer be ignored was read: two from General Washington, together with copies of twenty letters and papers from others detailing the dismal trend of events in Canada, where the American invading force had disintegrated. These letters created an unpleasant backdrop for a debate on independence. After further minor business, the delegates picked up the debate where they had left off.

One of the key arguments on Saturday had been that the plain people were not yet ripe for separation. Several of the delegates had spent Sunday gathering facts to prove the opposite, and when debate resumed on Monday they proceeded to read documents and letters from various colonies to show that the sense of the people favored independence. These readings convinced at least one of the wavering delegates—Joseph Hewes of North Carolina.

Joseph Hewes
AGE: 46   MERCHANT

Judgments varied. Hewes considered himself "a pence and farthings man" thrust by the times into politics. "A plain, worthy merchant," said one delegate, "[he] seldom spoke in Congress, but was very useful upon committees." Jefferson found him "very wavering, sometimes firm, sometimes feeble, according as the day was clear or cloudy." John Adams especially liked him. On the marine committee he and Hewes "laid the first foundations, the cornerstone of the American navy," he boasted. "Hewes has a sharp eye and keen, penetrating sense," he added, "but, what is of much more value, is a man of honor and integrity."

Hewes in a sense returned home when he came to Philadelphia to sit in Congress. He had been born across the Delaware River in Kingston, New Jersey, and after completing grammar school had been apprenticed to a merchant in Philadelphia. In his early thirties he migrated to Edenton, North Carolina, where he became a shipowner and merchant in partnership with a Scotsman named Robert Smith. (Through Smith he met another Scotsman named John Paul Jones, whose career in the American navy he helped launch; Jones always credited Hewes for getting him his first command.) In Edenton, he became "a particular favorite with everybody," regarded as "one of the best and most agreeable men in the world." He got engaged to a local girl; she died a few days before their wedding and Hewes never married. He stayed clear of politics until the Stamp Act, then followed a path others he would meet in Congress were traveling in their colonies: election to the legislature and when that was prorogued to the provincial congress, to the First Congress in 1774, and the Second in 1775.

Hewes arrived at the Second Congress willing to fight for American rights—he had forsaken the Quaker religion he had been reared in—but, he said, "we do not want independence; we want not revolution." During the year that followed his letters home reveal how events, not abstract political doctrine, drove this practical man of honor and integrity into a position he never dreamt of supporting.

June 5, 1775: I wish to God you was here that I might advise with you on some matters of great importance. . . . When a large extensive country loses its trade, when its ports are all shut up and all exportation ceases, will there be virtue enough found in that country to bear heavy taxes with patience? Suppose a country, no matter where, should be under such circumstances, and necessity should oblige the inhabitants to raise a large army for their defense, how is it to be paid? Suppose the exigencies of that country should demand *one million sterling per annum, how is it to be raised? How made? How sunk?*

December 1, 1775: No plan of separation has been offered; the colonies will never agree to any till drove to it by dire necessity. I wish the time may not come too soon. I fear it will be the case if the British ministry pursue their present diabolical schemes. I am weary of politics and wish I could retire to my former private station.

March 20, 1776: I see no prospect of a reconciliation. Nothing is left now but to fight it out, and for this we are not well provided, having but little ammunition, no arms, no money, nor are we unanimous in our councils. We do not treat each other with that decency and respect that was observed heretofore. Jealousies, ill-natured observations and recriminations take place of reason and argument. Some among us urge strongly for independency and eternal separation, others wish to wait a little while longer and to have the opinion of their constituents on that subject. You must give us the sentiment of your province when your convention meets.

By the end of March Hewes was exhausted emotionally and physically. Although two colleagues shared the burden of representing North Carolina, "I have been put on so many committees, some of a commercial kind, that I have a much harder time of it than either of my brethren." From April through June he alone spoke for his colony while Hooper and Penn visited home. During those three months he attended "some committee meeting every night and frequently in the morning before Congress meets," he said. "I have sat some days from six in the morning till five and sometimes six in the afternoon without eating or drinking."

Throughout the great debate on independence Hewes wavered until a reading of letters and resolution of public meetings in North Carolina convinced him the people were for it. Thereupon, John Adams said later, he "started suddenly upright, and lifting up both his hands to heaven as if he had been in a trance, cried out 'It is done! and I will abide by it.' I would give more for a perfect painting of the terror and horror upon the faces of the Old Majority at that critical moment than for the best piece of Raphael."

Hewes's change, satisfying as it was to Adams, worked no miracle. A test vote taken late in the afternoon of Monday, June 9, showed seven states—New Hampshire, Massachusetts, Rhode Island, Connecticut, Virginia, North Carolina, and Georgia—for immediate separation, and five—Pennsylvania, New York, Delaware, New Jersey, and South Carolina —against it. Maryland abstained. Though a majority favored independence all present knew that it could not be declared to the world until John Adams' thirteen ships, clocks, horses, or whatever had been aligned to move as one.

After the test vote discussion resumed, continuing once again past the usual adjourning hour and into the evening. At last, as darkness fell, an agreement of sorts was reached. Congress resolved that further discussion of independence be postponed for three weeks but "that in the meantime, lest any time should be lost in case the Congress agree to this resolution, a committee be appointed to prepare a Declaration. . . ."

The three weeks delay Edward Rutledge planned to request, but did not expect to get, had been granted in return for the right to begin at once preparing a declaration announcing America's decision to the world. The delay meant little unless within those three weeks the king's peace commissioners brought over an acceptable offer. If no such offer was forthcoming—John Adams was certain none would be —independence was all but a declared fact, assuming, of course, during that time a sharp shift of sentiment occurred among the delegates from the Middle Colonies. Not long after Congress had agreed to the postponement Oliver Wolcott of Connecticut, a sober, dignified gentleman seldom given to exaggeration, expressed in a letter to his wife what all his fellow delegates knew to be true: "We seem at present to be in the midst of a great revolution, which I hope God will carry us safe thro' with."

5

The Politicians

Professions are hard to pinpoint, but twenty-one of the Signers called themselves lawyers. There were also four physicians, one clergyman, an ironmaster, a retired printer, several merchants, a scattering of farmers, and a number who regarded themselves as country gentlemen. Looked at another way, there were a number in Congress who, regardless of how they earned their living, could only be called professional politicians. These were the men—led by Richard Henry Lee and Samuel Adams—who worked behind the scenes to shape congressional decisions. While a Chase or a Middleton sprayed invective from the floor the "pros" made policy.

The label "politician" must be used with caution. Nearly all the Signers had spent a large part of their adult lives in politics. They were accustomed to power. Every political post available in a colony without recourse to Britain had been held by someone in each delegation. Virtually every man over the age of thirty-five had been involved in the public affairs of his colony for at least a decade—most of them having been drawn into the arena by the Stamp Act. Franklin and Hopkins had first met at the Albany Congress in 1754; each had been in politics longer than the eldest man, (thirty-four years old) in the South Carolina delegation.

But the true politicians among these fifty-six gentlemen were a minority. A sense of duty had not carried them into public life. Politics was not a hobby with them nor an adjunct to their lives. It was their life. It swallowed up their days. Wheeling and dealing spiced all their waking hours.

The politicians among the Signers varied in temperament, from the solemn Samuel Adams to the good-humored Caesar Rodney, but all were intriguing characters. "I'm a terrible softie on most politicians, and I'm terribly fond of them," Russell Baker has said of a species that has come down to the present largely unchanged from the eighteenth century. "They're among the few people in America who still work, live by their wits, have no job security, endure brutal hours, and show great ingenuity even when they're thieves. They're the last people in America who go over Niagara Falls in a barrel—they take risks. Most of them have sufficient ambition to be extremely interesting; an evening spent with a politician is more entertaining than with just about anybody else."

No one fits that description better than Stephen Hopkins of Rhode Island, the dean of the politicians in Congress. In any sampling of the breed, Hopkins must lead the list.

$\mathcal{S}$tephen $\mathcal{H}$opkins
AGE: 69   POLITICIAN

Committee assignments lengthened every delegate's day. Usually the meetings were unwelcomed bores. An exception was the marine committee, created by Congress to buy and arm ships "for

the protection and defense of the United Colonies." Governor
Hopkins "kept us all alive," said John Adams:

Upon business, his experience and judgment were very useful.
But when the business of the evening was over, he kept us in
conversation till eleven and sometimes twelve o'clock. His
custom was to drink nothing all day, nor till eight o'clock in
the evening, and then his beverage was Jamaica spirit and
water. It gave him wit, humor, anecdotes, science, and
learning. He had read Greek, Roman, and British history, and
was familiar with English poetry, particularly Pope, Thomson,
and Milton, and the flow of his soul made all his reading our
own, and seemed to bring to recollection in all of us all we
had ever read. I could neither eat nor drink in those days.
The other gentlemen were very temperate. Hopkins never
drank to excess, but all he drank was immediately not only
converted into wit, sense, knowledge, and good humor, but
inspired us all with similar qualities.

Hopkins had been reared to be a farmer and an early marriage
at the age of nineteen, with the first of seven children soon on
the way, seemed to lock him into the ancestral mold. But he
refused to accept, as he was fond of saying, "the doctrine of
predestination" for himself or his God. He escaped from the farm
into surveying, and eventually bought a store in Providence that
led to a profitable career as a merchant. But the meat of his life
was politics, and when the marine committee heard him recite his
anecdotes he had already been practicing the art for forty-five
years, longer than anyone else in Congress. His career began when
he was twenty-four and the village of Scituate chose him to
moderate the town meeting, then the next year elected him town
clerk, and simultaneously sent him to the provincial assembly.
The assembly soon elevated him to speaker. Meanwhile, he developed a second career in the judicial system, starting as a justice
of the peace, moving on to the court of common pleas, then to
the superior court, where he became chief justice.

Rhode Island at that time had two political–commercial cen-
ters. Hopkins dominated the Providence area, and a youngster

eighteen years his junior, Samuel Ward, ruled the region around Newport. Hopkins became governor of Rhode Island in 1755. Two years later Ward shoved him from power, and from then on a war filled with corruption and ringing with slander raged between the two men, the battles sometimes ending with Hopkins in the governor's seat and sometimes Ward. A decade passed before they finally resolved to end the feud and thereafter concentrated their talents against the British.

The two traveled as a team to the First Congress but found that even on continental affairs they still viewed politics from opposite poles. Joseph Galloway of Pennsylvania introduced a plan of union for the colonies which, if Congress had accepted it, might have served as an opening wedge leading to reconciliation with the mother country. Ward opposed the plan. Hopkins, cautious, even conciliatory in his old age, favored it. "Met, considered of the right of Parliament to regulate trade," Ward noted in his diary after one session. "Mr. Hopkins for some of the modes proposed. I was for none." After the battle at Lexington, Ward came out bluntly for independence while Hopkins hung back. The cause and Congress lost Ward in March 1776 when he died of smallpox. (Ward at first thought he only had a hangover, for he had "spent the afternoon and evening as convivially as was common for him," his physician reported, but the next day "the smallpox came out by thousands in his face, which soon became one entire blister and in two or three days after the body and limbs were beset with such numbers of them that the load bore down his strength before it in spite of every measure taken for his assistance." He was fifty-one years old.)

Hopkins talked boldly in Congress—"the liberties of America would be a cheap purchase with the loss of but 100,000 lives," he told a colleague one day—but refused to commit himself on independence. He temporized, however, without offending those attached to the cause. By May he saw the decision was inevitable. "I suppose that it will not be long before the Congress will throw off all connection, as well in name as in substance, with Great Britain," he wrote home, warning his constituents, as a good politician must, what lay ahead. Six weeks later he cast his vote for independence.

The risks involved in the job of politics especially intrigued one of the Signers. "There is one ugly reflection," he said in a ruminating mood. "Brutus and Cassius were conquered and slain. Hampden died in the field, Sidney on the scaffold, Harrington in jail, etc. This is cold comfort. Politics is an ordeal path among red-hot plowshares. Who, then, would be a politician for the pleasure of running barefoot among them?" Roger Sherman for one, the man many of the delegates considered the supreme politician among the Signers.

Roger Sherman

AGE: 55   POLITICIAN

It embarrassed a colleague from Connecticut to have Sherman in the delegation to the First Congress. "Mr. Sherman is clever in private," he conceded, "but I will only say he is as badly calculated to appear in such a company as a chestnut bur is for an eye stone. He occasioned some shrewd countenances among the company, and not a few oaths, by the odd questions he asked, and the very odd and countrified cadence with which he spoke."

Odd was the word for Mr. Sherman. He was infuriatingly pious. "Mr. Sherman (would to heaven he were well at New Haven) is against our sending our carriages over the ferry this evening," a companion wrote, "because it is Sunday; so we shall have a scorching sun to drive forty miles in tomorrow." Once when Congress was backed up with business, it resolved to meet on Sunday. Mr. Sherman objected—out of "a regard of the commands of his Maker." After he heard that the continental army had been defeated on Long Island, although entrenched behind a chain of hills, he turned to a colleague and said: "Truly in vain is salvation hoped for from the hills and from the multitude of mountains."

He was odd and depressingly grave. To his face delegates addressed him as "Judge Sherman," but behind his back called him "Father Sherman." Once while absent from home he wrote his wife:

This is your birthday. Mine was the 30th of last month. May we so number our days as to apply our hearts to wisdom, that is, true religion. Psalm 90: 12.

> I remain affectionately yours,
> Roger Sherman

He disliked bawdy tales—"prognostiferous observations," he called them—and lived by such lugubrious sayings as: "Intestine jars are worse than foreign wars. . . . Plain downright honesty is the beauty and elegance of life. . . . All men desire happiness but 'tis only the virtuous that attain it. . . . The gods are slow but sure paymasters."

Then there was his deviousness. "But of my old colleague Sh——n, suffice it to say that if the order of the Jesuits is extinct their practices are not out of fashion," a victim remarked. The man "is as cunning as the Devil," said another, "and if you attack him, you ought to know him well; he is not easily managed, but if he suspects you are trying to take him in, you may as well catch an eel by the tail."

Odd! "Mr. Sherman exhibits the oddest shaped character I ever remember to have met with," said a delegate, attempting to sum up the man. "He is awkward, unmeaning, and unaccountably strange in his manner. But in his train of thinking, there is something regular, deep and comprehensive; yet the oddity of his address, the vulgarisms that accompany his public speaking, and that strange New England cant which runs through his public as well as private speaking make everything that is connected with him grotesque and laughable—and yet he deserves infinite praise —no man has a better heart or clearer head. If he cannot embellish he can furnish thoughts that are wise and useful. He is an able politician and extremely artful in accomplishing any particular object;—it is remarked that he seldom fails." That complimentary judgment seemed too temperate for Thomas Jefferson. "That is Mr. Sherman of Connecticut," he said one day, pointing out delegates to a visitor, "a man who never said a foolish thing in his life."

Connecticut could not be blamed for Sherman's "countrified cadence." He was born and reared in Massachusetts, trained there as a shoemaker, and not until the age of twenty-two did he travel —by foot with his tools and clothes on his back, according to tradition—to New Milford, Connecticut, where his older brother lived. He pieced out a living as a shoemaker and filled his "leisure hours in the study of *mathematics,*" then put the pastime to practical use as the county surveyor. He married at twenty-eight, when he felt prosperous enough to support a family. A year later he and his brother opened a general store in New Milford, and Sherman began publishing an almanac that contained his own astronomical calculations and "everything that I thought would be useful." His energy was endless. Angered at the depreciated paper money of neighboring colonies that the store had to accept at face value, he published *A Caveat Against Injustice, or an Enquiry into the Evil Consequences of a Fluctuating Medium of Exchange.* While running the store and preparing the annual edition of the almanac, he amused himself reading law. The year he turned thirty-four and began practicing law he handled one hundred twenty-five cases, kept a hand in the store, accepted election to the provincial assembly, served as a justice of the peace, and put out a new edition of the almanac.

This routine continued until 1760, when Sherman's wife died and left him with seven children to rear. Earlier he had opened stores in Wallingford and New Haven. After his wife's death he moved to New Haven and soon became the town's leading citizen —again a member of the provincial assembly, a justice of the peace, treasurer of Yale College, and, after a few years passed, judge of the superior court and member of the provincial council. He married again, this time to a striking young lady, twenty years his junior, who eventually added eight more children to his family.

Sherman opposed the Stamp Act but the "practice of great numbers of people assembling and assuming a kind of legislative authority passing and making resolves" against that act bothered him. He thought such assemblies would "tend to weaken the authority of the government" and "lead to such disorders and confusions as will not be easily suppressed or reformed." Opposition must follow the rules laid down in "our happy constitution." British imperial policy flouted those rules by taxing the colonists without their consent, but that did not justify similar disreputable behavior in the citizens of Connecticut. Parliament, as Sherman saw matters, had no right at all to legislate for the colonies in any way, even in the regulation of trade, and he carried that view down to the First Congress, where it was judged too radical to be respectable. News of the battle at Lexington pushed him even further out ahead of the pack. Soon after he arrived at the Second Congress he said that the delegates must "not neglect any probable means for a reconciliation with Great Britain" but that he had "no expectation that administration will be reconciled, unless the colonies submit to their arbitrary system or convince them that it is not in their power to carry it into execution."

This bold stand a year before independence did little damage to his reputation, which, now that Congress had become accustomed to his oddities, surpassed that of all members save possibly John Adams. He served on virtually every important committee created by the Second Congress, including the board of war, the marine committee, and the board of treasury. Among other principal assignments, a friendly compiler has remarked, "were those to prepare instructions for the operations of the army in Canada; —to establish regulations and restrictions on the trade of the United Colonies;—to regulate the currency of the country;—to purchase and furnish supplies for the army;—to devise ways and means for providing for ten millions of dollars for the expense of the current year;—to concert a plan of military operations for the campaign of '76;—to prepare and digest a form of confederation; —to repair to headquarters near New York and examine into the state of the army, and the best means of supply for their wants;

etc., etc." Naturally he was chosen to the committee created to draw up the Declaration of Independence. "He was so regular in business, and so democratic in his principles," an admiring delegate remarked, "that he was called by one of his friends 'a republican machine.' "

A few generalizations can be made about the politicians in Congress. More Northerners than Southerners made a career of politics and more men from New England than from the Middle Colonies. All, or nearly all, were mighty men within their colonies, but none ever achieved much of a reputation on the national scene. No man, except Benjamin Franklin, was better known or more admired within Pennsylvania and less known outside the colony than John Morton.

John Morton
AGE: ABOUT 52 POLITICIAN

A diversity of races and religions gave Pennsylvania politics a pungent flavor and chaotic character lacking in more stable colonies like Virginia. The diversity led John Morton to fear a specter other delegates worried little about. "We are preparing for the worst that can happen, viz., a civil war," he wrote a friend in England, shortly after the Second Congress had convened. "I sincerely wish a reconciliation; the contest is horrid. Parents against children, and children against parents. The longer the wound is left in the present state the worse it will be to heal at last." He would blame the British if his fears materialized. "You have declared New England people rebels, and the other provinces aiders and abettors. This is putting the halter about our necks, and we may as well die by the sword as be hanged like rebels. This has made the people desperate."

He used the Quaker "thee" and "thou" in letters and conversation, as a Pennsylvania politician had to, but traced his American roots back to a great-grandfather who had emigrated from Sweden to the Delaware Valley in 1654, and when he came to marry he chose a girl also descended from the Swedes who had first settled the region. He was born the son of a farmer and given virtually no formal education. He evaded the role predestined for him by becoming, with the help of a stepfather who taught him the craft, a surveyor, an escape route also used by two of his colleagues in Congress, Stephen Hopkins and Abraham Clark. As with them, the rod and transit provided a living, but politics gave flavor to life. He was elected to the provincial assembly in his thirties and served there for a decade. When he lost his seat, the governor appointed him high sheriff of Chester County, a post held until he worked his way back into the assembly, where he again became a fixture. In 1775 he was chosen by his peers to be speaker of the house. The previous year, though he had no formal legal training and only limited experience as a justice of the peace and president of Chester County's court of general sessions and common pleas, he was appointed to the colony's supreme court. It was a remarkable accolade. His colleagues on the bench were Chief Justice Benjamin Chew, rich, arrogant, and former attorney general of the province, and Thomas Willing, one of Philadelphia's wealthiest merchants.

The assembly chose Morton for the First Congress, where he renewed acquaintance with gentlemen met nine years earlier at the Stamp Act Congress. He rarely spoke from the floor. He and George Ross alone in the Pennsylvania delegation held that it would take more than petitions to cause the crown to change its policy toward the colonies, that economic coercion was needed. In the Second Congress he refused for many months to favor independence, yet somehow retained the respect of the faction that did. "Mr. Morton is ill," John Adams remarked one day, and because of his absence Pennsylvania's voice in Congress "has suffered by the timidity of two overgrown fortunes," John Dickinson and Thomas Willing. Later, his rectitude and skill as a moderator led to his selection as chairman of the committee of the whole during the great debates over the Articles of Confederation.

Britain's continuing refusal to conciliate America convinced Morton by the spring of 1776 that independence was inevitable. Events inside Pennsylvania, where plans were afoot to give the colony a democratic constitution, made him uneasy—a friend later said "Honest John Morton . . . died of grief at the prospect of the misery which he foresaw would be brought upon Pennsylvania" by her new constitution—but when the day came to vote for independence he cast his in the "aye" column. Less than a year later he was dead. "Tell them," he is supposed to have said on his deathbed of those friends who had abandoned him because of his vote, "tell them that they will live to see the hour, when they shall acknowledge it to have been the most glorious service I ever rendered to my country."

Any sampling of the politicians among the Signers must confront the peculiar case of Oliver Wolcott of Connecticut. Connecticut had yet to produce a more sure-footed political figure than Wolcott, and yet as a politician he had to be counted a failure.

Oliver Wolcott

AGE: 49   POLITICIAN

He "appears to be a man of integrity," a colleague wrote when Wolcott had spent most of his adult life in politics and nearly five years in Congress, "is very candid in debate and open to conviction and does not want abilities; but does not appear to be possessed of much political knowledge." He had the talent and experience to be a superb politician. He could excoriate a thin-skinned acquaintance offended "because he has not been treated with more particular marks of respect" by Congress, but in public he kept command of his temper, staying "as still as a mouse," he once told his wife, "and I hope you will not doubt my prudence." He came from the land of "blue laws" but held no prejudice against drinking. ("Paid General Wolcott my proportion towards four gallons of spirit," John Adams noted in his accounts when he, Wolcott, Whipple, and Lovell shared quarters in a boarding house.) Fellow delegates respected him enough to appoint him to the sensitive post of Indian commissioner for the Northern Department, where he acquitted himself admirably. Yet Wolcott never won the success in politics others less experienced and far less able achieved. The "great modesty" another colleague saw in the man, an unfitting quality for a politician, held him back. The in-fighting, the maneuvering required to rise to the top offended him. Whatever the vague phrase "political knowledge" meant, he lacked it.

Certainly he did not want for intelligence. At Yale he stood at the head of his class all four years. After graduation he studied medicine for a while, then ran for sheriff of Litchfield and won. He married the daughter of a sea captain from Guilford, Connecticut. It was a remarkably compatible union. He made his wife a partner of his public as well as private life. "My dear," he wrote from Philadelphia, "while I am here I shall mark the events, and if anything happens I shall give my opinion further upon it."

Wolcott rarely lost a political post until elevated to a higher one. The job as Litchfield's sheriff (held for twenty years) was the cornerstone upon which he built his life in public affairs. While holding it he was elected to the provincial assembly (served four terms), became a major in the local militia (eventually promoted to general), was selected for the colony's council (fifteen years in office). Along the way he also served as judge of the court of probate in Litchfield (for nearly a decade) and judge of the county court (four years in office). He joined the Second Congress in 1775 and missed attending only one year until the Revolution ended.

Wishful thinking seldom clouded Wolcott's political judgments. His letters from Philadelphia reported what he thought, not necessarily hoped, would happen. "A final separation between the countries I consider as unavoidable," he told his wife in April 1776. "My Dear," he wrote in mid-June, "we seem at present to be in the midst of a great revolution, which will probably be attended with most important consequences. Everything is leading to the lasting independence of these colonies." Not long after writing those words he did a curious thing. On Friday, June 28, the day Jefferson laid his Declaration before Congress, he left for Connecticut, although he knew that on the following Monday, July 1, the final debate on independence would commence. He assumed the issue was not in doubt. He had been away from home over six months. He knew his substitute, William Williams, was on the road to Philadelphia. Still, to depart then resembled leaving a great play before the curtain dropped. It showed a lack of dramatic sense, a serious defect in a politician. Clearly, as his colleague said, Wolcott did not possess "much political knowledge."

When he returned to Congress on October 1, 1776, rested and in good health again, Wolcott signed the Declaration.

6

A Look around
the Room

It was an elite club that never met with all members present. Never were the fifty-six men who signed the Declaration together in one room at the same time. But the act of signing that document gave them a bond that allows them to be treated together.

None of these gentlemen were teetotalers and several were heavy drinkers of spirits as well as wine, but without exception they never, so it was said, drank "beyond the limits of propriety." The typical Northerner at the time of the signing was forty-nine years old. The Southerners, notably younger, averaged out to thirty-eight years. The Northerners would live longer. Only four of the twenty-four Southerners would see seventy, while ten of the fourteen New Englanders and nine of the twenty-one members from the Middle Colonies would live past that age.

All but three of the Signers were married. The bachelors spread themselves evenly the length of the continent—Joseph Hewes representing the South, Caesar Rodney the

Middle Colonies, Elbridge Gerry New England. (Gerry married later at the age of forty-two, time enough to father seven children.) The Southern delegates tended to marry young, two-thirds of them before twenty-five, while more than three-fifths of those from the North waited until after that age to make the move. Benjamin Rush, speaking for other self-made men in the North, said no woman would "tempt him to perpetrate matrimony till he had extended his studies so far that a family would be no impediment to his farther progress"; he wed only after he had turned thirty and established himself as a physician in Philadelphia.

Benjamin Rush

AGE: 30   PHYSICIAN

He was "a comely young man," with a slender frame that would thicken only slightly through life, had "highly animated" blue eyes, an expressive face seldom seen in repose, and an "uncommonly large" head which "bespoke strength and activity of intellect." He could be rash—"prudence," he was fond of saying, "is a *rascally* virtue"—self-righteous, and impetuous, but never a bore. He shared much in common with his friend John Adams. Both sprang from families that had "lived without tumult or luster." Both liked to talk and wrote easily in a relaxed, lively style. They loved equally to argue—"he dares not dispute nor contradict me," Rush once said of a companion, "and this is not only the life of conversation but steel to the flint of genius"—and quarreled with all who saw the world differently. Both envied the well-to-do and yearned for rank and place. What had once been said of Adams—he "could not look with complacency upon any man who was in possession of more wealth, more honors, more knowledge than himself"—could have been said of Rush. Self-pity suffused much of what they said and wrote. When Adams observed, "I have had poverty to struggle with, envy and jealousy and malice of enemies to encounter, no friends, or but few, to assist me," he expressed a sentiment Rush had penned many times.

The early death of his father left Rush to be reared by a stepfather he disliked and a mother who ran a grocery store. His mother forced upon him a solid Presbyterian education. After graduating from the College of New Jersey, he toyed with the thought of becoming a lawyer, but when told lawyers were no more than abusive pettifoggers he switched to medicine, saying "to spend and be spent for the good of mankind is what I chiefly aim at." After an apprenticeship under a reliable Presbyterian physician in Philadelphia, the family scrounged up enough money to send him to the University of Edinburgh, then on to London for some practical experience in the hospitals there.

At Edinburgh Rush paused long enough from his medical studies to persuade Mrs. John Witherspoon—whose refusal to risk her life on the ocean blocked her husband's acceptance of the presidency of the College of New Jersey—that the waters of the reputedly tempestuous Atlantic, which he had recently spent several storm-tossed weeks upon, were rarely ruffled by wind or rain. Rush might be "a most agreeable young man," said Witherspoon as he watched his wife being charmed out of her fears, but his addiction to "strong and superlative expressions" gives reason for no little "uneasiness." In London, between medical lectures and tours of the hospital wards, the newly anointed M.D. visited the House of Commons, that "cursed haunt of venality, bribery, and corruption!" Benjamin Franklin, whom he had once blamed for the Stamp Act ("O, *Franklin, Franklin,*" he had said in 1765, "thou curse to Pennsylvania and America, may the most accumulated vengeance burst speedily on thy guilty head!") now became a revered friend. Franklin advanced the money that let him visit Paris before returning home. French women proved "very beautiful," though Rush noticed it took considerable "painting" to achieve the effect. It fascinated him "to see them take out a little box of paint, which they always carry in their pockets, together with a small looking glass, and a fine pencil, and daub their cheeks over in their coaches, when they are going to

A Look around the Room 69

an assembly or any public entertainment." He had less to say in his journal about the leaders in medicine, science, and politics that Franklin's letters of introduction allowed him to meet.

He returned home "resolved to be a great man." He began building a medical practice in Philadelphia, lecturing on chemistry at the College of Philadelphia, and churning out a stream of medical papers that he hoped would win him election to the prestigious Royal Society in London. An essay on slavery carried him into public affairs. Why the sudden urge to talk about slavery? "Remember," he said, "the eyes of all Europe are fixed upon you to preserve an asylum for freedom in this country, after the last pillars of it are fallen in every other quarter of the globe." Slavery is a crime against God and man, and "national crimes require national punishments," he warned. Extravagant statements came naturally to Rush. If the East India Company were allowed to land its tea in America, "then farewell American liberty!" he told the people of Philadelphia shortly after publishing his essay on slavery. "We are undone forever." Those chests of tea "contain something worse than death—the seeds of SLAVERY. Remember, my countrymen, the present era—perhaps the present struggle—will fix the constitution of America forever. Think of your ancestors and of your posterity."

Rush circled on the periphery of the First Congress, getting to know most of the delegates socially but having no part in their decisions. "He is an elegant, ingenious body. Sprightly, pretty fellow," John Adams wrote in his diary. "But Rush, I think, is too much of a talker to be a deep thinker. Elegant, not great." But by the time the Second Congress met he was calling Rush "a worthy friend of mine," "a gentleman of an ingenious turn of mind, and of elegant accomplishment." Adams was ten years older than Rush, an experienced politician, and except for James Wilson the best-read man in America on the theory and practice of government. Rush became his political protégé after the British marched on Lexington. Shortly after Rush had been chosen a member of Pennsylvania's new delegation to Congress Adams met him on the street and offered congratulations. Rush said the new members would face every issue with uncompromising honesty. Adams smiled and said that to praise a politician's honesty "is saying a great deal of a public character, for political integrity is the rarest virtue in the whole world."

Rush became a zealous supporter—possibly the first prominent man in Philadelphia to do so—of independence from the day he heard of the British march on Lexington. "Britain and America *will* hereafter be distinct empires," he predicted. "America is the *punctum saliens*—the only vivid principle of the whole world." However, he kept his zeal restricted to friends and pseudonymous newspaper articles. He explained why when encouraging a new friend named Thomas Paine, whom he had met at a local bookstore, to write a pamphlet on the subject. "I suggested to him," Rush said later, "that he had nothing to fear from the popular odium to which such a publication might expose him, for he could live anywhere, but that my profession and connections, which tied me to Philadelphia, where a great majority of the citizens and some of my friends were hostile to a separation of our country from Great Britain, forbade me to come forward as a pioneer in that important controversy." Paine "seized the idea with avidity." When done, he entitled his work *Plain Truth*. Rush suggested *Common Sense,* and the pamphlet came out under that title on January 9, 1776, two days before Rush, at the age of thirty, married Richard Stockton's daughter Julia.

Through the first half of 1776 Rush used every moment he could spare from patients to take on any assignment that might promote acceptance of independence among the people. The leaders "rely chiefly upon me," he wrote his wife in May, paused over the boast, lined out "me" and added "Colonel McKean and a few more of us for the salvation of this province." His efforts were rewarded with election to Congress on July 20. He took his seat there two days later. "I find there is a great deal of difference between sporting a sentiment in a letter or over a glass of wine upon politics," he said, "and discharging properly the duty of a senator. I feel myself unequal to every part of my new situation except where plain integrity is required." That humility vanished quickly. On his second day he spoke for ten minutes on the proposed Articles of Confederation, emboldened by an awareness that "even our illustrious body is marked with features of human nature. We can talk nonsense now and then as well as our neighbors. This reconciles me to myself."

But Congress and Rush never became reconciled to one another. Colleagues liked him—"Dr. Gay," as Thornton nicknamed him, "tripped round, sung a tune, and told me 'all would end well' "—but they constantly suggested by allusions to his profession, which they seldom made about the three other physicians in Congress, that his calling was medicine, not politics. "The learned doctor . . . labors under a spasm," Richard Henry Lee, once a good friend, said during one debate, and in another he wished "the learned doctor would distinguish between the practice of children and men." Innocence, compounded with impatience scotched his chance to succeed in politics. "Patience! Patience! Patience!" John Adams told him, is the "first, the last and the middle virtue of a politician," but Rush could not heed the admonition. The war must be won in a day. "Pray don't let this matter be neglected," he told one colleague; "our salvation hangs upon it." Handle this matter "in an *instant,*" he ordered another; it must not be "debated and postponed in the usual way for two or three weeks." A friend's promotion "must not be neglected," the "clothing and officering of the army" must be dealt with immediately. When Congress dallied, Rush concluded that "the *vis inertiae* of the Congress has almost ruined the country."

It could be said of Rush as he said of himself, "he aimed well." It could also be said he had no business being in Congress. It surprised no one and perhaps relieved many to see him one of the first dropped from the Pennsylvania delegation. He never again in a long, useful life filled an elective office.

Married or not, most of the delegates lived as men without women while attending Congress. Though none were poor, few except John Hancock and some Southerners could afford the luxury of bringing their wives to Philadelphia, the most expensive spot on the continent to live. Also, most of them still had children at home for their wives to tend. The burden of congressional duties left little time for the pleasures of family life.

The delegates might have been isolated on an island for all the chance they had to enjoy the pleasures of civilized life. They lived largely unto themselves, their days—often their evenings—swallowed up by business. "I have sat some days from six in the morning till five and sometimes six in the afternoon without eating and drinking," one member reported. Even in their free time members rarely escaped from shop talk. Jefferson lived alone in a small apartment; Hancock rented a spacious house, as did Harrison and a few other Southerners; but most of the delegates settled with colleagues in boarding houses scattered about the city. At first each colony's delegation tended to live unto itself, but as Congress got to know itself the members regrouped. John Adams ended sharing quarters with William Whipple of New Hampshire, while his cousin Samuel roomed with Roger Sherman of Connecticut and Matthew Thornton of New Hampshire. Delegates continued to vote by colonies and to fight against any decision that infringed upon their colonies' interests, but by the summer of 1776 personal ties, cutting across sectional and provincial boundaries, counted for much. John Penn of North Carolina served as the mouthpiece for Robert Morris of Pennsylvania when Morris was absent from Congress. Edward Rutledge of South Carolina grieved when his friend John Jay of New York could not make it back to Congress in time to fight against the Declaration. Not once did Benjamin Rush of Pennsylvania speak on the opposite side of a question from his friend John Adams. The day Congress edited the Declaration found Jefferson sitting not among his colleagues from Virginia but next to Benjamin Franklin. William Floyd had been born and reared on Long Island but all his friends were New Englanders.

William Floyd

AGE: 41   FARMER

Floyd appeared out of place in the New York delegation, a farmer of little education, "not at all gifted with suavity of manner," but coupled by political accident during his years in Congress with such suave New Yorkers as James Duane, John Jay, and Alexander Hamilton. He had been born and reared on Long Island, technically part of the colony of New York, but with cultural and economic ties to New England that dated back to the days when its first settlers had migrated from there. Floyd would not have hesitated to call himself a transplanted New Englander. He was a "rigid" member of the Congregational Church living in a colony dominated by Anglicans. Most of his financial dealings were with friends and business acquaintances in Connecticut; the Trumbull family there had long owed him a large debt still being paid off in 1776 in painfully small installments. During the First Congress he was quick to make friends with members from Massachusetts, with whom he felt more at ease than with his colleagues from New York. Two years later when the British invaded Long Island and occupied his house he retreated, not to New York, but to Connecticut where he lived out the war.

Floyd excelled neither as an orator or as a politician. He served on few important committees in Congress. He was a mild man, undistinguished in intelligence or in appearance, except, to judge from his tailor's bills, by the fine clothes he wore. There was a final flaw: he alone among his brethren from New York was an early opponent of reconciliation with Great Britain and had "always voted with the zealous friends to liberty and independence."

For all this, the delegates from New York trusted him completely, often for months at a time leaving him as their single spokesman in Congress. He may have been plodding and colorless, but no faction could seduce his vote with flattery. His conduct has "gained him much respect in Congress," John Jay reported back home, and although Jay might not like some of his principles, Floyd "appeared always to judge for himself" on any issue that did not require him to betray either his instructions or the interests of New York. Though an unremarkable man who preferred to talk about hunting, a passion with him, rather than politics, his career as a congressman in a day of rapid turnover, especially in the New York delegation, would be remarkably long —from the opening session of the First Congress to the end of the Revolution.

Floyd sprang from a line of farmers that stretched back to the early seventeenth century, when the founder of the American branch of the family emigrated from Wales. In keeping with tradition, he had received a plain education that, it was hoped, would hold him tied to the soil. From the home base in Suffolk County, Long Island, his father had built what *he* had inherited into a comfortable fortune, and Floyd, when eighteen, carried on as was expected of him. By the time of the Stamp Act he was the richest man in the county and lived according to his means. He owned a dozen or more slaves, and nothing in the words "freedom" and "liberty" then being bandied about persuaded him to free them. (He still owned eleven Negroes in 1795.) He was well liked. The men in his company elected him colonel of the local militia. After the British occupied Long Island, they ordered the trees on his land cut down for use as firewood in New York City. Tradition has it that "not a laborer turned out."

Probably because he alone could afford the trip to Philadelphia, the county sent him to Congress, from where he prodded friends at home toward bolder resistance against the British. He predicted in May 1776, while other New Yorkers still talked of reconciliation, that "we have little or no hopes" for peace from commissioners rumored to be on their way from England, and "therefore we ought to be in a situation to preserve our liberties another way." The hints did no good. In July, New York's instructions still forbade her delegates to vote for independence, and Floyd agreed "faithfully [to] pursue them." Later in the month the instructions were changed. Floyd, that "mild and decided republican," was the first in his delegation to place his name upon the embossed copy of the Declaration.

Outside Congress the delegates appeared as a congenial group of easy-going gentlemen. Within, personal differences often led to bitter explosions. "We grow tired, indolent, captious, jealous and want a recess," one member reported in December 1775. The sarcasm and personal aspersions that Middleton of South Carolina and Chase of Maryland injected into debate often left their targets shaking with fury.

Arthur Middleton

AGE: 34 COUNTRY GENTLEMAN

He was rich, handsome, cultivated, and hot-tempered—the personification of the Southern gentleman of fiction. He owned over two hundred slaves and a house full of Italian paintings—more likely reproductions—picked up on a Grand Tour of Europe. "He had been educated in England and was a critical Latin and Greek scholar," said an awed colleague who had mastered neither language. "He read Horace and other classics during his recess from Congress." He was a private man, with the same quiet reserve of his father, Henry Middleton. While he possessed "the plainest manners with the most refined taste," a contemporary said, "his temper was violent, and it is evident he had it not under perfect control." He could not be bothered with trifles. When Congress elected him to the committee of accounts, he refused to serve, saying that he "hated accounts, that he did not even keep his own accounts, and that he knew nothing about them."

When twelve years old his father sent him to be educated in England. He remained there nine years, ending up reading law at the Middle Temple. He returned home to find his mother dead, his father remarried, and three sisters born in his absence. He did what was expected of him—married, then accepted the political duties a gentleman must bear, first as a justice of the peace, then as a member of the legislature. Middleton played the role for four years, but when the boredom became intolerable he and his wife went to Europe. They lived there for nearly three and a half years. A son, named after his father, was born in London, the first of nine children. Back in South Carolina the family settled at "Middleton Place," a plantation on the Ashley River. Middleton built two wings on the old house to accommodate his proliferating family. One day while out for a walk a servant rushed up with a message from Mrs. Middleton: the roof of the main house was on fire. Her husband looked around, saw no danger of the fire spreading to the wings, said "let it burn," and walked on. (Mrs. Middleton, the teller of the tale adds, "did not view the thing quite so coolly, and took the necessary measures to have the fire extinguished.")

With the European holiday over, Middleton dutifully re-entered the legislature. There, despite affection for the mother country, he warmly defended American rights. Indeed, "the temporizing spirits, and those who were 'infirm of purpose,' complained that Mr. Middleton hurried them on too rapidly; and that he always advocated what were termed desperate measures." When Henry Middleton returned from the First Congress with news that the colonies had created an Association, whereby all trade with England would cease until American grievances had been redressed, his son said that those who refused to sign the Association should be excommunicated from Carolina society, that the property of those who fled the colony should be confiscated, and that "he looked without disfavor on such activities as the tarring and feathering of Loyalists."

Arthur Middleton did not join the Second Congress until mid-May 1776, but he quickly made his presence felt. "He spoke frequently, and always with asperity or personalities," a delegate remarked. "His speeches were short, and he usually delivered them under the influence of strong feelings." Only a short time passed before he and John Adams tangled. "He had little information and less argument," Adams recalled. "In rudeness and sarcasm his forte lay, and he played off his artillery without reserve. I made it a rule to return him a Roland for every Oliver, so that he never got, and I never lost, anything from these reencounters. We soon parted, never to see each other more—I believe, without a spark of malice on either side; for he was an honest and generous fellow, with all his zeal in the cause."

Middleton came to Philadelphia determined to oppose any compromise with Great Britain but also to delay a declaration of independence until the timing seemed right. He resisted independence up to the last moment but on July 2 changed his mind with great reluctance and voted for it.

Samuel Chase

AGE: 35   LAWYER

His mother died when he was a child, leaving him to be reared and educated by his father, a clergyman in the Anglican Church who had emigrated from England to a congregation in Baltimore too small to provide a decent living. Father and son did not get along. Later Chase did nothing to deter a mob that sought to force his father, among others, to take a loyalty oath to Maryland's new government. When Congress moved to Baltimore in 1777 delegates heard that the old man was "not so zealous a Whig as the son," and that he still preached and spoke as he thought.

Chase put his father and Baltimore behind him at the age of eighteen, moving to Annapolis, where he would live until after the Revolution. He read law there and was admitted to the bar when twenty years old. He entered the profession with impressive credentials for one so young: a sound grounding in the classics; an ability to blend zeal with eloquence when pleading a case; a quick mind and a sharp tongue; and enough self-confidence to be intimidated by no one. He was a tall man, standing over six feet, and big-boned. He had a large head and a reddish countenance that caused colleagues to nickname him "Bacon Face." He was "ever social and talkative" and this, along with his apparent integrity, helped to win the friendship of the sedate William Paca. "His person and manner were very acceptable," said a colleague in Congress who did not like him, "and to these he owed much of his success in political life."

Political life for Chase began when he was twenty-three. Assuming the role of a democrat, a man of the people, he promoted as candidates for the town council of Annapolis, up to then the preserve of the local elite, a shoemaker, a carpenter, a tailor, and a grocer, and in the process got the town to send him to the provincial assembly. His shenanigans at the time of the Stamp Act led the mayor of Annapolis to denounce him as "a busy, restless incendiary . . . a ringleader of mobs . . . a foul-mouthed and inflaming son of discord and faction . . . a common disturber of the public tranquillity." Chase replied in kind. He dismissed his opponents collectively as "despicable pimps and tools of power," then got down to cases: one man had a "passion for wealth," another a *"revengeful temper,"* another favored "harlots' embraces" as well as *"vice and folly, drunkenness and debauchery,"* and still another excelled at *"cringing* and *fawning* and *pimping* and *lying."*

Chase kept this invective up for a decade. Years later he gave some advice to a son-in-law. "You are a democrat; and you are right to be one, for you are a young man," he said. But an old man, he went on, "would be a fool to be a democrat." On that point Chase seems never to have been a fool. Even as a young man he kept democracy at a distance. He agitated for his own ends, not the people's, using them to supplant the current "establishment" with a new generation of the elite. Long before he became old he worked to block the people from power. "We have found by experience that giving the choice of officers to the people is attended with bad consequences," he said early in Congress. He hedged Maryland's constitution of 1776 with enough checks virtually to stifle the voice of the people in government.

In the First Congress Chase appeared erratic but not radical. In one breath he could oppose conciliatory gestures of those for reconciliation and in the next announce: "I am one of those who hold the position that Parliament has a right to make laws for us in some cases, to regulate the trade . . . and in all cases where the good of the empire requires it." In the Second Congress he continued to be an amiable companion out of doors but within "violent and boisterous," tedious "upon frivilous points," and absolutely unpredictable. "It is the maddest idea in the world to think of building an American fleet," he said one day, then reversed himself a few months later. He never hesitated to offend anyone who thought other than he. A friend of one of his targets once said in a rage that except for the fact that he was in Congress "I would not set very tamely" listening to such insults. The comment did not daunt Chase. "I think the gentleman ought to take offense at his brother delegate," he said, not Samuel Chase. But when someone tried to humor him from an extravagant position, he was offended. "The gentleman is very sarcastic and thinks himself very sensible," he replied to one such attempt.

Reactions to Chase among the delegates were mixed. "He possessed more learning than knowledge, and more of both than judgment," said one; "a bold disclaimer with slender reasoning powers." John Adams found him tedious in debate but also "very active, eloquent, spirited, and capable." He once dared to reprimand Chase's "impudence," but that outburst came only after the debate on independence. Until then he had to be handled warily, for as Chase went so went Paca and the Maryland vote. While "he was generally with us," his vote could never be certain until cast.

In February 1776 Congress assigned Chase, with Franklin, Father John Carroll, and Charles Carroll of Carrollton, to the delicate task of wooing Canada into the fold as the fourteenth colony. He returned to Congress in mid-June with word the mission had failed. He left at once for Maryland to see his "extremely ill" wife and to prod the provincial convention into giving its delegation in Congress permission to vote for independence. "I have not been idle," he reported back. "I have appeared *in writing* to the people. County after county is instructing." The field work put enough pressure on the Maryland convention that the instructions to the congressional delegation were changed to permit a vote for independence. Chase failed to make it to Philadelphia in time to cast his vote. "I hope ere this time the decisive blow is struck," he wrote to John Adams on July 5. "How shall I transmit to posterity that I gave my assent?" Adams replied immediately. "As soon as an American seal is prepared, I conjecture the Declaration will be subscribed by all members which will give you the opportunity you wish for, of transmitting your name among the votaries of independence."

Middleton and Chase were two of a number of gadflies Congress had to contend with. Members found it harder to classify Robert Treat Paine. Sometimes he seemed a gadfly, sometimes a misfit who had no business being in Congress, sometimes only a confused, unsure gentleman who had yet to find himself.

Robert Treat Paine
AGE: 45 LAWYER

He alone among those from the North who signed the Declaration had a middle name, a distinction rare to virtually all of eighteenth-century America. (Respect for the family tree set in only after the Revolution, when suddenly and for no clear reason children the length of the land began to sprout middle names.) Robert Treat had been the first governor of Connecticut, and Paine proudly pointed out his grave in Milford, Connecticut, when the Massachusetts delegation traveled to the First Congress. The attempt to live up to the name he inherited helped to account for the trouble Paine had finding himself in life. He once said he had "neither health enough for an active life nor knowledge enough for a sedentary one." Whatever the reason, he ended up being something less than he should have been.

He was reared in comfortable circumstances in Boston, the son of a former clergyman who had achieved what looked like a successful career in business when Paine was born. The boy went the usual route for a well-bred youngster in Boston—seven years at the Latin School, then on to Harvard, class of 1749. Everything came easy to his quick, clever mind and his agile hands. Too easy. For a time he would seek "after a minute and particular knowledge of mathematics," break away from that to learn French, drop that to devise an ingenious alarm clock or to practice painting on glass. He said he "took more pleasure in solving a problem in algebra than in a frolic," but when the frolic came along Paine preferred that. He was a tall, gaunt youngster, a marvelous storyteller, and equally popular with classmates and the girls of Boston. Even John Adams, who did not like him ("he is an impudent, ill-bred, conceited fellow") confessed "he has wit, sense, and learning, and a great deal of humor and has virtue and piety, except his fretful, peevish, childish complaints against the disposition of things."

The disposition of things turned against Paine in college. His father's business fell apart, and a lad who expected to take over the family business found himself after graduation teaching in a country village. When the farmers pumped him for political news from the city, Paine—"O, how I laughed in my sleeve"—gave back "very learned and elaborate answers" sprinkled with "words and expression without meaning" about topics "I did not understand." He lasted out the school term, then began a life of peregrination that extended nearly seven years. He tried to peddle goods from a hired boat along the coastal creeks of North Carolina. The country bumpkins there did not take his jesting lightly. "About one o'clock this morning," he reported, "a pack of drunken fellows came on board and among other abuses threw a black quart bottle of rum at my head." The bottle struck a glancing blow but "stunned me so that I could hardly walk all day." Next, he sailed for Philadelphia with a cargo and came down with smallpox. He went back to North Carolina again seeking fortune as a merchant, but the disposition of things remained against him. He sailed aboard a chartered sloop to the Azores and Spain, then on a whaling vessel bound for the waters off Greenland. Later, when he learned that but one lawyer served the district of Maine, then a part of Massachusetts, his thoughts turned to a new direction. He settled down to read law in the office of a country attorney, glad at last, he said, to be free of the "impertinencies of a city life." An invitation to serve as a substitute preacher for a congregation in the neighborhood diverted him once more. He asked his family not to "divulge about this extraordinary undertaking"—a temporary job he explained. During the French and Indian War he tried for an army commission. Failing that, he signed on as an army chaplain for a three-month tour of duty. The tour led to a winter at Lake George which produced little to joke about. He came down with "a very bad cold," he said; "praying and preaching abroad in very thick and raw cold air" proved "very prejudicial to the head." After leaving the "suffocating smoke" of army campfires behind, Paine next tried surveying; then came another stab at the law. Though he still found it hard to concentrate on one project—between part-time duty as a salesman for cannons made by a local foundry he experimented with an electrical machine, and there were always girls for the bachelor to squire and frolics to attend—Paine was admitted to the bar two months after his twenty-sixth birthday. The same week his father died, passing along to his son the chaotic remains of his business.

The disposition of things continued bad for Paine. Boston had a surplus of lawyers and after four unprosperous years he moved out of the city to the outskirts of the colony—as had James Wilson and George Ross in Philadelphia—to the town of Taunton. There he did well. When the Stamp Act came, Paine opposed it in a loud voice and said that to defeat it "he would go to make brass knuckles." An acquaintance agreed "he might do that to great advantage, for his stock would cost him nothing." Little was heard from him during the next four years. He courted the daughter of a local tavern keeper and on March 15, 1770, at the age of thirty-nine, married her. Two months later she bore him a son. Soon afterward Paine was called to Boston to serve as prosecutor of the British soldiers involved in the Boston Massacre. John Adams defended the men. Adams won. It rankled Paine to be defeated by a stodgy upstart four years his junior. The jury in the case was rigged to acquit, but if Paine knew this he never remarked upon it.

Taunton elected him to the legislature three years later, and there his voting record satisfied the Whig majority enough to send him to the First Congress in Philadelphia, although his commitment to the cause lacked enough warmth to satisfy Samuel Adams. "He was moderate in his feelings for his country," a colleague in Congress said. "This was so much the case that he told me the first time I saw him in 1774 that his constituents considered him one of their 'cool devils.' " He admitted to friends he dreaded "the mad rage of unrestrained liberty full as much as the arbitrary imposition of uncontrolled power."

The Second Congress enjoyed his wit out of doors but winced when he took the floor within. "He had a certain obliquity of understanding which prevented his seeing public objects in the same light in which they were seen by other people," a delegate remarked. "He seldom proposed anything, but opposed nearly every measure that was proposed by other people, and hence he got the name of 'The Objection Maker.' " Off the floor and around the committee table he proved "eminently useful" and "remarkable for his regular and punctual attendance."

He and John Adams kept their distance in Philadelphia. When Adams proposed George Washington for commander in chief, "Mr. Paine expressed a great opinion of General Ward and a strong friendship for him." When Adams pressed for independence, Paine temporized. When Adams asked for ideas on the form Massachusetts' government should take after independence, Paine kept silent. When Adams was elected chief justice of Massachusetts' newly created superior court and Paine only to a justice's seat, Paine resigned, causing Adams to remark smugly that "the bench will not be the less respectable for having the less wit, humor, drollery, or fun upon it; very different qualities are necessary for that department."

To his credit, Paine hung on, kept up a working relationship with John Adams, tended to his committee assignments, and showed up when the time came to vote for independence. "Paine has been very ill for this whole week," Adams wrote shortly before the day arrived to sign the Declaration, "and remains in a bad way. He has not been able to attend Congress for several days, and if I was to judge by his eye, his skin, and his cough, I should conclude he never would be fit to do duty there again, without a long intermission, and a course of air, exercise, diet, and medicine. In this I may be mistaken." He was. Six days later Paine signed the Declaration. He stayed in Congress until December, and though he asked only for a leave of absence "after laboring in the service sixteen months without cessation" he never again returned.

That the delegates endured day after day the likes of Chase, Middleton, and Paine, that they found the strength under relentless pressure to keep their sanity through the long sessions and endless committee meetings, owed something to the presence in their midst of a small band of good-humored gentlemen. It was hard to decide who should be included in this group. Certainly Caesar Rodney and Stephen Hopkins belonged there, but as men who had made a career of politics they were expected to have a way with a tale and an eye for the humorous aspect of things. One of the drollest men in the room was a lawyer named James Smith. He added nothing substantially to the stature of Congress or contributed much to the shaping of the great decisions, but he did have a way of easing tension with a story.

James Smith

AGE: ABOUT 57   LAWYER

Colleagues thought him "a pleasant, facetious lawyer" and had little else to add, but in time he would be remembered as "perhaps the most eccentric character" among the Signers. He was born in northern Ireland and came when about ten years old to Pennsylvania with his family. He went to school, under a sound Presbyterian clergyman, where Latin and Greek were balanced with a practical course in surveying. He read law in the office of his brother at Lancaster and under the lax standards of the day was admitted to the bar when twenty-six years old. He then moved out to the frontier, settling in among the Scotch–Irish. There he pieced together a living as a surveyor who handled legal problems on the side. There, too, he met George Ross, another young bachelor lawyer, known, like Smith, for his sometimes "obstreperous mirth."

Around 1750 Smith settled in the village of York. The Pennsylvania Dutch prevailed there and throughout the county. Normally they had little use for Scotch-Irishmen like Smith, who drank heavily—he was "fond of the bottle" according to one contemporary; "he loved wine, and drank much of it," another said—and had a light-hearted attitude toward religion. (He attended Sunday morning service regularly but dodged the afternoon meeting because "a second sermon in the same day always puts the first one entirely out of [my] head.") But for some reason they tolerated Smith's eccentricities. He prospered as a lawyer. He stayed a bachelor until after he had turned forty, and then married a girl from New Castle, Delaware, the home town of George Ross. She was twenty years his junior.

Smith's "original species of drollery" did much to relieve the dreary solitude of York. "In him it much depended on an uncouthness of gesture, a certain ludicrous cast of countenance, and a drawling mode of utterance, which taken in conjunction with his eccentric ideas, produced an effect irresistibly comical," said one of his admirers. "The most trivial incident from his mouth was stamped with his originality, and in relating one evening how he had been disturbed in his office by a cow, he gave inconceivable zest to his narration, by his manner of telling how she thrust her nose into the door, and *there roared like a Numidian lion.*"

Smith "was never so successful as when he could find a learned pedant to play upon," notably Judge Charles Stedman, who, "when mellow, was best calculated for his butt." Stedman was a Scotsman and also "a man of reading and erudition, though extremely magisterial and dogmatical in his cups." When the judge was displaying his learning, Smith could always "set him raving by some monstrous anachronism."

"Don't you remember, Mr. Stedman," he remarked gravely one evening, "that terrible bloody battle which Alexander the Great fought with the Russians near the Straits of Babelmandel?"

"What, sir!" said Stedman with unconcealed contempt, "which Alexander the Great fought with the Russians? Where, mon, did you get your chronology?"

"I think you will find it recorded, Mr. Stedman, in Thucidydes or Herodotus."

"On another occasion," said a visitor from Philadelphia temporarily shunted to York, "being asked for his authority for some enormous assertion, in which both space and time were fairly annihilated, with unshaken gravity he replied, 'I am pretty sure I have seen an account of it, Mr. Stedman, in a High Dutch almanac printed at *Aleepo,*' his drawling way of pronouncing Aleppo. While everyone at the table was holding his sides at the expense of the judge, he, on his part, had no doubt that Smith was the object of the laughter, as he was of his own unutterable disdain. Thus everything was as it should be, all parties were pleased; the laughers were highly tickled, the self-complacency of the real dupe was flattered, and the sarcastic vein of the pretended one gratified; and this, without the smallest suspicion on the part of Stedman, who, residing in Philadelphia, was ignorant of Smith's character, and destitute of penetration to develop it."

Smith showed little interest in politics for a long while. He concentrated on his family of five children, his law practice, and on a venture in iron manufacturing run for him, he said after losing £5000 in it, by one man who "was a knave, and the other a fool." When Parliament closed the port of Boston as punishment for dumping tea in the harbor, he called for a ban on all imports from Britain until colonial grievances were redressed. He also raised a volunteer company of which, when expanded into a battalion, he was elected colonel. While Congress debated independence in June 1776, Smith was in Philadelphia attending a conference of men from all parts of Pennsylvania who favored independence. The conference began in "a spirit of harmony"; then "some small bickering between Colonel Smith of York County and the members of Chester County" broke out. This time Smith's humor failed to soothe, for in the dispute "Elisha Price of Chester got beside himself so far that he run in the yard, jumped over the fence, so into the street, where he was pursued, took to his lodgings and continued so as not to be capable to attend again."

Back in York, Smith did his best to stifle sentiment for reconciliation. When Judge Stedman showed up with a petition opposing independence, Smith saw orders "issued forthwith for securing Mr. Stedman's portmanteau, and keeping an eye on his person, till he might be examined." Stedman departed with his petition unsigned and under "such circumstances as caused two young men who came with another large packet of these treasonable papers . . . to decamp with precipitation."

In July 1776 Smith represented York County at a convention called to draw up a constitution for Pennsylvania. During the first week members chose him for the delegation to supplant Pennsylvania's old one in Congress. He took time out to sign the Declaration, but otherwise gave Congress little attention until the constitutional convention finished its work at the end of September.

Among the fifty-six men who signed the Declaration Button Gwinnett of Georgia had the honor to represent the black sheep of America. Hardly anyone could be found who had a good word to say for him.

$\mathcal{B}$utton $\mathcal{G}$winnett

AGE: 41   BANKRUPT LAND SPECULATOR

He was born in England, the son of a Welsh clergyman and an English mother, married when twenty-two, emigrated to Georgia when thirty years old. He came with enough money or goods to set up as the proprietor of a country store in Savannah. Three years later he purchased St. Catherine's Island, a block of land ten miles long off the coast of Georgia and near the town of Sunbury. He bought the island and the slaves to cultivate it on credit, without a shilling down payment. From that day on he lived mired in debt. He made a perfunctory attempt to assume the responsibilities of a country gentleman, accepting an appointment as justice of the peace and election to the provincial assembly, but he spent most of his time in these and the following years attempting to extricate himself from debt. Early in 1773 pressure from creditors forced him to declare bankruptcy. Undaunted, he tried to sell off parts of the island, although he no longer owned it, to innocent immigrants. One man bilked by him censured "his base designing views," and it was generally agreed that Gwinnett's "honesty was far from great."

Gwinnett's financial shenanigans did not deter friends in the assembly from electing him to Congress. He accepted the honor reluctantly; he wanted to stay home and seek glory on the battlefield as commander in chief of the Georgia militia. Gwinnett and Lyman Hall traveled together to Philadelphia and took their seats in Congress on May 20, 1776. Since both were warm for independence, those for the cause judged them "intelligent and spirited men, who made a powerful addition to our phalanx." Later it became apparent Gwinnett "was of an irritable temper and impatient of contradiction," and, what was worse to some, "a zealous democrat." His fellow Georgian, George Walton, detested him.

Gwinnett wanted to leave for home directly after casting his vote for independence, although he had been in Congress less than a month and a half. He was persuaded to linger long enough to sign the embossed copy of the Declaration but was so eager to set out for Georgia that on the day of the signing Congress allowed him to be the first to place his name on the paper. The haste to get home was wasted. Thanks in part to Walton he failed to get the coveted military post. His "irritable temper" led to a duel in which he died May 16, 1777.

Gwinnett alone in Congress represented the bankrupt in the country. Those delegates not born to wealth had, except for Samuel Adams and Abraham Clark, neither of whom coveted money, prospered enough to be called well-to-do.

Approximately half the Signers had received a college education in America or its equivalent abroad. Also about half knew Europe at first hand. Franklin had spent sixteen years in England, with time off for visits to Scotland, Ireland, Holland, France, and Germany. Middleton knew Italy; Carroll had spent several years in France; and Lewis' business had carried him as far as the northern parts of Russia. Foreign travel may or may not have influenced their decisions in Congress, but as a gentleman of a later day once said, "if one has lived much of his life abroad, as I have, one is apt to judge his country more precious than do those who know no other country well."

These gentlemen in 1776 did not consider themselves servants of the people. They had been chosen by their local assemblies, or, if the assemblies had been prorogued, by the royal governors, by provincial conventions or congresses. But even if the people had elected them, the delegates, by reasoning that prevailed in the eighteenth century, were still their own men. "You assert that there is a fixed intention to invade our rights and privileges," a group of inhabitants told Benjamin Harrison as he was about to leave for the First Congress; "we own that we do not see this clearly, but since you assure us that it is so, we believe the fact. We are about to take a very dangerous step, but we confide in you, and are ready to support you in every measure you shall think proper to adopt."

Members of Congress arrived at decisions behind closed doors, and once they had decided what was best for the country it was the people's duty to accept what their betters had resolved.

And the delegates on the whole *were* better men, among the best America had to offer in 1776.

7

The Mild and Steady

The men who shaped the content of the Declaration of Independence and who in the long run gave the character to the American Revolution were not gadflies like Chase or even strategists like Samuel Adams and Richard Henry Lee. The bulk of Congress was composed of solid and serious gentlemen who rose about six in the morning, attended committee meetings until Congress convened, sat in Congress until three or four in the afternoon, then, after dining and an hour or two of relaxation attended committee meetings in the evening. Among these mild and steady gentlemen the most overworked were the merchants.

They varied as men and in their views on independence, but a common experience in business caused them to be among the hardest working members of a Congress that lacked a bureaucracy to carry out its directives. State papers were written by others while these gentlemen searched for ways to supply the navy with ships and crews, the army with shoes and food and cannon balls.

$\mathcal{G}eorge$ $\mathcal{C}lymer$
AGE: 37 MERCHANT

"A cool, firm, consistent republican who loved liberty and government with equal affection," said a member of Congress who believed George Clymer to be one of the wisest men, Benjamin Franklin excepted, he had ever known. "Under the appearance of manners that were cold and indolent, he concealed a mind that was always warm and active towards the interests of his country. He was well informed in history, ancient and modern, and frequently displayed flashes of wit and humor in conversation." All in all, "a great mass of genius, knowledge, and patriotism, without the least portion of party spirit, will descend with him to the grave."

He gave the world "a pleasing countenance" and to colleagues in Congress seemed a gentle as well as a genteel man. He was not, however, to be trifled with and "never patiently submitted to any indignity." Once, when convinced he had been unfairly ridiculed by a piece in the press, he went to the printer's office "and bestowed upon him a severe and well-merited chastisement with his cane," an acquaintance recalled. "His notions of independence and right were not abstractly confined to national affairs, and he always demanded towards himself that politeness and respect which he was ever careful to show others." He did not judge friends by their politics. Thomas Paine was a frequent and welcomed guest, but he did not share a number of Paine's democratical notions. Clymer believed that "a representative of the people," as he was fond of saying, "is appointed to think *for* and not *with* his constituents." After he had been elected to an office he "showed a total disregard to the opinions of his constituents when opposed to the matured decisions of his own mind."

Clymer's parents died when he was one. As with Hancock, an

uncle who was also a wealthy merchant brought the boy into his home and reared him. The uncle, William Coleman, had, according to his friend Franklin, "the coolest, clearest head, the best heart, and the exactest morals of almost any man I ever met with." His large library and band of intellectual friends gave Clymer a taste for books and philosophical discussion he never lost. But a living had to be made and, as an acquaintance put it, "he entered the compting-room of his uncle for the purpose of acquiring a knowledge of mercantile pursuits." He disliked business and its "peculiar precariousness," but he excelled at it. The year of the Stamp Act he married Elizabeth Meredith, daughter of a merchant, and that led to another partnership, a commercial one with his father- and brother-in-law, and also to a friendship with a young man from Virginia named George Washington, who often visited the Meredith home.

Early in the 1770s Clymer's eldest son died, and this "for a long time embittered his existence." While the wound healed he channeled much of his great energy into the opposition against Great Britain. He headed the committee created to prevent the landing of the East India Company's tea in Philadelphia. After the battle at Lexington he became one of the first of the city's leading citizens to come out for independence. His probity allowed him to hold this radical view without losing the confidence of moderate men. In July 1775 Congress appointed him one of the two continental treasurers. He soon afterward committed his purse to the Revolution by exchanging all his gold and silver for continental currency. He further underscored faith in the cause by purchasing loan certificates, both those issued by Pennsylvania and by Congress, to the limit of his ability. (At the Constitutional Convention in 1787 he turned out to be the fourth largest holder of these certificates.)

In May 1776 Clymer ran for the Pennsylvania Assembly on a platform that called for an immediate declaration of independence. He alone of the four candidates on his ticket won. In July he was chosen to help draft a constitution for Pennsylvania, but the convention sent him instead to Congress. He took his seat on

July 20. The delegates, who already knew of his executive ability through his work as treasurer, immediately handed him a number of demanding committee assignments. He realized "his dearest wish," he said, the day he signed the Declaration of Independence. The British would make him pay for the fulfillment of that wish. When they later occupied Philadelphia, they looted his house.

Philip Livingston
AGE: 61   MERCHANT

On the eve of independence there were four members of the Livingston clan in Congress: Philip, his younger brother William (fifty-three years old), young John Jay (thirty-one), married to William's daughter, and the still younger Robert R. (thirty). Philip and William came from the branch of the family that belonged to the Presbyterian Church; Robert and John Jay were Anglicans. But blood and background united where religion might have divided. All worked hard down to the end for reconciliation with England. Colleagues questioned which of the four most irked those in Congress who agitated for independence. It was probably Philip.

"In his temper Mr. Livingston was somewhat irritable," a charitable contemporary remarked. "There was a dignity, with a mixture of austerity, in his deportment, which rendered it difficult for strangers to approach him, and which made him a terror to those who swerved from the line, or faltered in the path of personal virtue and patriotic duty." A final observation—"he was silent and reserved, and seldom indulged with much freedom in conversation"—failed to fit the man known to Congress. There he was neither silent nor reserved, although he did not converse. He "is a great, rough, rapid mortal," said one member. "There is no holding conversation with him. He blusters away." He could be embarrassingly blunt. Once when someone leaked a secret of Congress he proposed that every member publicly swear he had not been the guilty party. In that way, he said, "the rascal might add the sin of perjury to that of treachery and thereby damn his soul forever." He detested "the levelling spirit" of New England. He dreaded independence because once cut adrift "we should go instantly to civil wars among ourselves to determine which colony should govern all the rest."

Livingston came from an aggressive, acquisitive clan long accustomed to power and wealth. He was born on the family manor near Albany, graduated in the class of 1737 from Yale, married a socially acceptable well-to-do girl from Albany, then set up in business as an importer in New York City. Family connections coupled with intelligence and energy quickly brought him a fortune. He lived in a handsome house on lower Manhattan except during the torrid summers when the family moved to a country house across the East River on Brooklyn Heights. With money enough to satisfy him, Livingston branched out. He had a hand in founding the New York Society Library, the St. Andrew's Society, the city's chamber of commerce, the New York Hospital, and King's College. To all these ventures he brought a blustery drive slightly softened by something akin to good-humored tolerance. He could be a rigid Presbyterian when fighting Anglican control of King's College, then the next moment contribute to the building of a Methodist meeting house or pause to censure the people of Massachusetts for persecuting Quakers. He could slip a scatological passage into a political pamphlet one day and on another endow a chair in divinity at Yale.

As he approached forty, Livingston eased into politics as a member of the city's board of aldermen. Four years later he moved on to the provincial assembly where he joined the ancient battle between the colony's two great families, the DeLanceys and the Livingstons, a battle for power in which neither side seemed concerned with what was best for the colony. Livingston reacted predictably to the Stamp Act: he opposed it and also the riots that resistance to it had occasioned. He was among those chosen to represent the colony at the Stamp Act Congress, where he met several gentlemen who would later turn up in the Second

Congress, among them McKean and Rodney. The assembly chose him speaker in 1769. After failing to reconcile differences with the DeLanceys—he feared that the split among the elite might permit the radical Sons of Liberty to take control of the colony—he was defeated for re-election. From outside the legislature he worked with one hand to smother the Sons of Liberty and with the other wrote and spoke steadily against British oppression. The assembly sent him and his brother William to the First Congress. He accepted all that body's measures, although the nonimportation agreement imposed serious financial losses upon him. In the Second Congress he served on several important committees, among them the marine committee, the committee on Indian affairs, the committee on commerce, and the treasury board. "He was very useful," a delegate said, "in committees where a knowledge in figures or commercial subjects was required."

The views Philip Livingston carried into the Second Congress were summarized by his cousin in a letter written three days after Lexington and Concord. "Every good man wishes that America may remain free," Robert R. Livingston, Sr., said; "in this I join heartily; at the same time I do not desire she should be wholly independent of the mother country. How to reconcile their jarring principles, I profess I am altogether at a loss." Philip and the three other congressional members of the clan held that view down to the day Congress voted for independence. Once the decision had been made all four, good politicians who could bend to reality, abandoned their position. When the day came to sign the Declaration, Philip alone of the clan was in Congress. He signed for the family.

Francis Lewis

AGE: 63 MERCHANT

One delegate dismissed him in a line—"a moderate Whig, but a very honest man, and very useful in executive business"—and no one else had much more to add. Though a good man, another member remarked, "he seldom quits his chair to speak." He buried his personality in silence. His letters read like an auditor's reports. He personified the stereotype of a businessman—solid, dependable, hard-working, dull—and seemed incapable of dramatizing the life he had led. No one appeared aware that he had seen more of the world, led a more adventurous existence than anyone in Congress. He had twice been shipwrecked on trips to Europe. He knew Russia better than perhaps any American, and had visited all her seaports from St. Petersburg to Archangel. He had been captured during the French and Indian War and escaped with his life only because, so he thought, the Indians believed him to be one of them, assuming that the Welsh he spoke was the dialect of a distant tribe. The French knew better, and when he was turned over to them they sent him to France where he was eventually exchanged.

Lewis did not emigrate to America until he was twenty-five years old. He had been born in Wales, the son of a minister. Both father and mother died when he was a child. A maiden aunt in comfortable circumstances took the orphan into her home. She insisted he learn Cyrmic, the Welsh language, sent him to Scotland where he picked up Gaelic, then to the Westminster School in London. Upon graduation he was apprenticed to a London mercantile house. In his early twenties he inherited a modest amount of property which, with the gambler's boldness that marked his life, he converted into merchandise and took along when he sailed to New York City. There he sold his cargo at enough profit to set up a business. When thirty-one he married a local girl. He retired from business at the age of fifty-two, "one of the most opulent men in New York."

In the years following the Stamp Act Lewis dabbled enough in politics for people to know he did not like Parliament's attempts to legislate for the colonies, but not until after the Boston Port Act did he take an active part in the opposition. He was soon known as one of the city's "leading radicals," a man who "would speak and act effectively and unhesitatingly for radical measures."

His wealth and rectitude, however, made him acceptable enough to more moderate men so that they did not object when he was selected to be a delegate to the Second Congress.

Congress always passed over Lewis when forming a committee to deal with matters of policy, but when it wanted a practical problem solved it turned to him. In September 1775 he was chosen "to purchase £5,000 worth [of] coarse woolen goods for the use of the Continental Army." In October Congress thought it "expedient that I should proceed" to New York "in order to purchase necessaries for the troops at Cambridge." In February 1776 "Mr. Lewis engaged to procure shoes for part of the army," a delegate reported. "He has had a parcel made in Jersey because cheaper than elsewhere." While others agonized over independence, Lewis searched for a way "to forward to General Washington at Cambridge the five tons of powder now at New Brunswick."

Lewis would probably have preferred Congress to delay a declaration of independence until further attempts at reconciliation had been made, but once convinced of the practical advantages of separation he gave his assent. His loyalty to the cause was deep and strong. When his daughter married a British naval officer, he ceased to speak to her. A month after he signed the Declaration the British ransacked his house, destroying books, papers, and furniture, and they imprisoned his wife. She was exchanged, but the experience shattered her health, and she soon died.

Nearly all the Southern delegates and perhaps half those from the North considered themselves country gentlemen, but most of them only lived in the country while the law or politics or business absorbed the bulk of their energies. Several of these gentlemen, however, though they differed widely in temperament and outlook, were alike in that they were completely satisfied to be country gentlemen and nothing more. Duty alone rather than a love for politics or power brought them into public life and carried them into Congress. There they made no great mark, though they generally did well whatever work was assigned them. They left when the first honorable excuse came their way: Lewis Morris and Carter Braxton in 1776, Arthur Middleton in 1777, and Francis Lightfoot Lee in 1779. All four felt much as Lee, who exemplified the breed, when he remarked, "What damned dirty work is this politics!"

Francis Lightfoot Lee

AGE: 41   COUNTRY GENTLEMAN

A relaxed attitude toward life allowed him to do his duty without making a career of it. He was educated at home by tutors, but instead of going abroad for further study, as his brothers did, he settled on an estate in Loudoun County received from his father. It was said that "from the earliest entrance in life he was addicted more to pleasure than business," but he did serve for a decade in the House of Burgesses without a break, a quiet, unobtrusive member notable only for his early and firm resistance to British policy after the Stamp Act. He waited until the age of thirty-five to marry. After the wedding he moved to a plantation in Richmond County, where his wife had been reared. Richmond returned him as regularly to the legislature as Loudoun had. He was sent to Congress in 1775, and sat there silently, as he had in the House of Burgesses. Those who watched how he voted and listened to his conversation in private were impressed. He "possessed, I thought, a more acute and correct mind" than his brother, said one member. "He often opposed his brother in a vote, but never spoke in Congress. I never knew him wrong eventually upon any question."

He came to Congress favoring independence but saw no reason to hurry the decision along. "You may be assured," he told a friend in April 1776, "the question has never been before the Congress, and it is probable they will wait till the people bring it before them." He did not agonize over the decision to break with the mother country. The issue was simple and clear-cut for him. "I feel myself deeply interested in the security and happiness of America, compared with which the interests of Britain is a feather in the scale," he said, putting briefly what Richard Henry Lee took hours of orating to state. Nor would he worry about the future that independence would bring to America. "Let us, my dear friend, do the best we can for the good of our country, and leave the event to fate."

The majority of the gentlemen who signed the Declaration defy any category except that of the mild and steady.

They made little noise, even in the most tumultuous debates. None had a flamboyant personality, although Walton was known for his warm temper. They were not necessarily dull men, only unobtrusive. They had another characteristic in common: all were quiet but firm supporters of independence.

Josiah Bartlett
AGE: 46   PHYSICIAN

It could be said of Bartlett, as indeed a colleague in Congress did, that "he was ignorant of the world." It could also be said that he looked at the world through his own eyes. In Amesbury, Massachusetts, where he was born and reared, he served five years as an apprentice to a local physician, who indoctrinated him with the prevailing theory that disease resulted from the accumulation of "morbific matter" in the body. Purge the system of these elements and health would be restored. Some physicians favored bleeding, others strong emetics, and still others a scientific blend of the two. It was also generally accepted that the "putrid matter" that caused a fever could be perspired away by isolation in a hot, closed room. Two years after Bartlett had moved to Kingston, a town in southern New Hampshire, to start his own practice, he came down with a blazing fever. "At the approach of the crisis his strength was so much exhausted by a warm and stimulating regimen and seclusion from the air, that his physician pronounced his disorder fatal," an acquaintance who got the story from Bartlett reported, "but the patient prevailed upon two young men that night to procure for him a quart of cider, which he took by half a teacupful at a time, by which he was so invigorated that in the morning a copious perspiration ensued, and his fever was effectually checked. Ever after this event Dr. Bartlett was a strict observer of nature in all diseases, and rejecting all arbitrary rules, he founded his practice upon the details of nature and experience."

His independent thinking carried over into religion. He was a deist, but few of the country people he served as physician and politician knew this. "He was sensible that no prejudices were so strong as those excited by religious tenets," a friend in on the secret said, "and that, if his opinions were generally known, they would render him unpopular. He therefore not only used great caution in concealing them, but paid taxes to the minister of the town in which he lived, and often attended his preaching."

Four years after migrating to Kingston Bartlett wed a cousin from Massachusetts. His wife was soon busy rearing the first of twelve children, while he concentrated on an increasingly prosperous practice. The Stamp Act carried him into politics and to the provincial legislature. The Wentworth family through a virtually hereditary hold on the royal governorship—no living man could remember when a Wentworth had not been governor—dominated New Hampshire's political life. Bartlett established himself at once in the assembly as an opponent of the family's almost regal authority. The governor tried to buy his allegiance, as he had others, with his appointment as justice of the peace, then as a colonel in the militia. Bartlett accepted both posts and continued his opposition.

His political career in the 1770s fit the mold of others he would meet in Congress: election to the provincial committee of correspondence, to the provincial convention, to the First Congress, to his colony's committee of safety, and to the Second Congress. He failed to attend the First Congress because his house had recently burned down, set on fire, rumor had it, by a gang of Loyalists. ("Some renegade Tories," it was said, "of the class then called 'cow boys,' may have composed this band.")

Colleagues in Congress judged him a man "of excellent character, and warmly attached to the liberties of his country." Behind those clichés lay an embarrassingly shy man who never gave a speech in Congress. "He seldom saw company, except on business," a friend said. "He visited but a few, and seldom invited any person to visit him. Many people complained that they did not know *where he lived.*" He was notorious for his frugality. "When judge of the superior court," a friend recalled, "he sometimes traveled fifty miles a day without eating, except the biscuit he had in his pocket, or baiting his horse—and they both slaked their thirst in the running brook. In traveling as delegate to Congress he refused to drink wine, and declined paying his [share] of the expense with his fellow members."

Through the early months of 1776 Bartlett alone represented New Hampshire in Congress, a burden "too weighty and important to be left to one man," he wrote home, or at least "too much for me." He explained the need for help: "There are four or five standing committees appointed, some for secrecy, some for dispatch, some of which are entrusted with large powers, and that there may be no cause of complaint they have appointed one delegate from each colony on each of these committees. Two or sometimes three of these committees set at the same time, so that tho' I almost every night and morning before and after Congress attend the business, yet our colony is sometimes not represented when some business of consequence is transacted by said committee."

When William Whipple arrived to share the load, Bartlett took a holiday but returned in time to hear the debate on independence. Tradition has it that "when the vote for independence was taken his name was first called, as representing the most easterly province, and he boldly answered in the affirmative." Possibly, too, the voice quavered, for Bartlett was exhausted. "I have not been able to attend either the Marine or Secret Committee for some time past, and Congress but little," he wrote not long after signing the Declaration. "By the advice of my friends and physicians, I design to leave this city in a few days, and try to move homeward."

It was said of Bartlett that "having formed an opinion he adhered to it with great tenacity," but at least once during the Revolution he faltered. "Mankind in general are such infernal and ungrateful beings," he told William Whipple during a weak moment, "that it seems but right that nine-tenths of the world should be kept in order by force." Whipple, who often bolstered the faith of others, would not tolerate such talk from a friend. "The disposition you have shown in opposition to tyranny and monarchical government convinces me of the impossibility that you can really entertain sentiments repugnant to every principle of republicanism." No further words of doubt and despair were heard again from Bartlett.

Lyman Hall
AGE: 52 PHYSICIAN

Hall, like Hooper of North Carolina, spoke with a New England accent. Though he had lived in the South for nearly twenty years, he left no one in doubt he came from Connecticut and had been "strongly impressed with the principles and habits of republicanism" that prevailed in that colony. Once, when he alone represented Georgia in Congress, a Southerner complained that "Georgia always votes with Connecticut and is no other use in Congress." Only when the sometimes ill Walton returned to his seat did the Southerner "perceive that Georgia is now frequently divided when any question relates to colonial politics," for "these two delegates are of different principles or different judgments."

Hall came originally from Wallingford, Connecticut. He went to Yale—class of 1747, a year behind Lewis Morris—and expected to become his parents' tithe to the church. He was ordained a Congregational minister after graduation and accepted a call to the pulpit in the village of Fairfield. He and his country congregation did not get along. When twenty-seven years old, he was charged with immoral conduct. He confessed the charge was true, repented with a sincerity that impressed his elders, and was restored to the ministry. The following year he married a Fairfield girl. He continued to eke out a living filling vacant pulpits as a substitute minister while using his free time to prepare for another profession—this time medicine. His wife died as he was beginning to practice as a physician in Wallingford. When he remarried it was to another girl from Fairfield. For reasons unexplained the newlyweds soon joined a group of New Englanders who over a half-century earlier had migrated to South Carolina.

Hall and his wife arrived in South Carolina to find the displaced New England community—350 whites and 1500 blacks—moving to supposedly lusher soil along the coast of Georgia. It took little time to learn that the settlers had calculated badly. The town of Sunbury that they founded in the parish (Georgia's equivalent of a county) of St. John lay on the edge of a string of swamps, which, though good for growing rice, were infested with malarial mosquitoes. Hall prospered as a physician, and soon owned a rice plantation and two of the choicest lots in Sunbury. And the transplanted community survived. By the eve of the Revolution it harbored one-third of Georgia's tiny population.

Georgia, with only fragile ties to her twelve sisters, hung like a satellite on the edge of the American empire, the last of the colonies to be founded, the least developed. The turmoil that stirred the other colonies from the Stamp Act onward barely penetrated its swamps and clearings. Most of the settlers, if they thought about politics, were satisfied with the royal governor and his rule; they voiced few complaints about their place in the empire. Only in St. John's parish, packed with "descendants of New England people of the Puritan independent sect," as the governor complained, did the citizens grumble about British oppression. When the Georgia legislature refused to recognize the nonimportation agreement promulgated by the First Congress, St. John's parish, led by Hall, seceded from the colony and in

February 1775 applied to the committee of correspondence of Charleston for "permission to form an alliance with them. . . ." Charleston rejected the appeal of the parish, whereupon the political orphan voted to send Hall to the Second Congress as "the delegate from St. John's."

Hall served in Congress from May through August 1775, listening and sometimes contributing to the debates but unable to vote since he represented only *"part* of a province." He impressed colleagues as "a man of considerable learning, with an excellent judgment, and very amiable manners." Also as a handsome man, standing "about six feet high and finely proportioned," but, said one observer, "the ascendancy which he gained sprung from his mild, persuasive manner, and calm, unruffled temper" rather than his imposing presence. Hall was absent from Congress through the early months of 1776. By the time he returned, St. John's parish had rejoined Georgia, and he came now as a legitimate delegate authorized to vote. He arrived back in Philadelphia May 20, accompanied by Button Gwinnett, and when the day came cast his vote unhesitatingly for independence.

Thomas Heyward, Jr.

AGE: 30   LAWYER

The men who represented South Carolina in Congress prided themselves on their individuality. But with the personalities stripped away, the bare bones of their lives revealed them as stereotypes cast from nearly identical molds, their records, with only a change here and there, as interchangeable as the spokes of a wheel. Heyward—or "Haywood" as delegates invariably misspelled it because he and fellow Southerners pronounced the name that way—is a case in point.

VITA

Birth: July 28, 1746, son of a wealthy planter.
Education: At home by tutors and in England, where he en-

tered the Middle Temple when nineteen.

Career: Admitted to South Carolina bar 1771; elected to provincial assembly 1772; married 1773 to the daughter of a wealthy planter; served in provincial convention 1774; elected to provincial congress and to council of safety 1775; elected to Second Continental Congress February 16, 1776; chosen for committee to draw up a constitution for South Carolina, which was adopted March 26, 1776; took seat in Congress April 24; signed Declaration of Independence five days after his thirtieth birthday.

Religion: Church of England.

Character: "Of good education and most amiable manners"; "not insensible to wit and pleasantry"; "a man of candor and integrity."

Hobby: Writing poetry, or as a colleague in Congress put it, "he possessed poetical genius, which he sometimes exercised with success upon various events of the war."

There is little in this vita to distinguish Heyward from his colleagues Middleton, Lynch, or Rutledge. All were about the same age, were educated abroad, worshipped in the same church, and had nearly identical political careers. But here, as with Thomas McKean, the mystery of personality enters in. For Heyward alone in the South Carolina delegation came to Congress in favor of independence. There is no other way to explain John Adams' admiration for the man. "On him," said Adams, "we could always depend for sound measures, though he seldom spoke in public."

Samuel Huntington

AGE: 45   LAWYER

Later, months after he had signed the Declaration and served as President of Congress, Huntington impressed a delegate who had little good to say for any of his other colleagues. He "is a man of mild, steady, and firm conduct and of sound methodical judgment," he wrote, "tho' not a man of many words or very shining abilities. But upon the whole is better suited to preside than any other member now in Congress." Huntington sensed his lack of "shining abilities" and compensated in a notably New England way: "his distinguishing characteristics were brevity and caution."

He was born in Windham, Connecticut, of a family of farmers that traced itself back to the first generation of New England settlers. He was apprenticed to a cooper when sixteen. During his free time as an apprentice and journeyman cooper he taught himself Latin and studied the available law books in town. He was admitted to the bar at the age of twenty-seven. He practiced for a time in Windham, then moved to Norwich, less than a day's ride away but a larger town on the busy Connecticut River. Confidence in his ability to earn a living as a lawyer led him the following year to return to Windham long enough to marry the minister's daughter.

His life in politics began in 1764 with election to the provincial assembly. In the year of the Stamp Act he became a justice of the peace and the king's attorney for Connecticut. He also joined the Sons of Liberty of Norwich, making him one of two members in Congress at the time of the Declaration—William Ellery was the other—who belonged, or admitted they belonged, to that radical revolutionary group, as it would later be judged. This dubious association—he never boasted of it in later years—was enhanced by a further accolade in 1765, election to the colony's council when he was thirty years old. Only a man who blended brevity with caution could have managed so many distinctions in a single year.

In a colony noted for thrifty citizens, Huntington was known to be parsimonious. "We found him," said a visitor to his rooms in Philadelphia one evening, sitting by the light of "a single candle." The visitor added: "It is said that he is hardly more enlightened, figuratively speaking, than he is in the literal sense of the word, but he is an upright man, who espouses no party, and may be relied on." Although the self-made son of a farmer, he was no man of the people. "His manners were somewhat formal," it was said, "and he possessed a peculiar faculty of repressing impertinence, repelling unpleasant advances, and keeping aloof from the criticizing observations of the multitude."

Neither penuriousness nor aloofness diminished his success in politics. In the decade after the Stamp Act he served quietly on the council without attracting attention to himself or his views. A month after the battle at Lexington he was put on a committee to organize Connecticut's defenses. Five months later the legislature sent him to the Second Congress, and after a tortuous journey across rivers filled with ice and roads clogged with snow he reached Philadelphia in mid-January 1776. He spoke seldom from the floor, did his committee assignments with dispatch, and offended no one, though it was known he favored independence. "A sensible, candid, and worthy man," said a member who signed the Declaration with him.

Thomas Nelson

AGE: 37   COUNTRY GENTLEMAN

The father wanted something better than William and Mary College for his son. When Nelson was fourteen he sent him to England to be educated, and there he stayed until he was twenty-one. The years abroad left their mark. "By his long residence in England, he had acquired in a considerable degree, an attachment to the manners of its country gentlemen, and a fondness for their pursuits," a contemporary said. "He rode out daily to his plantation, a few miles from York, a servant generally attending him with his fowling piece, and in the winter exercised himself in company with his friends and neighbors once or twice a week in a fox chase."

While Nelson was still at sea on the ship bringing him back home, York County elected him, sight unseen, to the House of Burgesses. Three years later he was elevated to the council, an adviser to the governor at the age of twenty-five. Then came the Stamp Act. Despite his affection for things English, he thereafter sided with his friend Thomas Jefferson against every British attempt to tax the colonies.

A delegate in the Second Congress gave a blunt but fair judgment of Nelson: "a fat man" but also "a speaker and alert and lively for his weight." He left Congress in late February 1776 to attend the provincial convention in Virginia, and there he helped force through a resolution that asked Congress to declare the colonies independent states, to seek foreign alliances, and to form a confederation. Nelson carried the momentous resolution to Philadelphia and there turned it over to Richard Henry Lee, who as senior member of the colony's delegation introduced it to Congress on June 7. Later, after Nelson had signed the Declaration, he told a colleague "that he was the only person out of nine or ten Virginians that were sent with him to England for education that had taken a part in the American Revolution. The rest were all Tories."

William Paca

AGE: 35   LAWYER

"I walked a long time this morning backward and forward in the State House yard," a delegate wrote in his diary in September 1775. His companions were William Paca and Thomas Johnson, Jr., of Maryland, and Thomas McKean. "McKean has no idea of any right or authority in Parliament. Paca contends for an authority and right to regulate trade, etc." So Paca contended, but the words he spoke only echoed his alter ego Samuel Chase. Delegates deplored the close tie between Paca, "beloved and respected by all who knew him," and the "violent and boisterous" Chase. Paca, said one, was "a good tempered worthy man, with a sound understanding which he was too indolent to exercise. He therefore gave himself up to be directed both in his political opinions and conduct by Samuel Chase, who had been the friend of his youth and for whom he retained a regard in every stage of his life." As a result, Paca's "reputation in public life was less than his talents."

It was an odd friendship built on contrasts. Chase was homely and ungainly, Paca suave and "not merely a fine looking man, he was handsome." Chase was parochial; until the Revolution he had never traveled beyond Maryland's borders. Paca's prosperous father sent the boy to the College of Philadelphia, class of 1759, then, after two years in an Annapolis law office, on to London for two years at the Inner Temple. Paca returned home to marry a girl with "a very considerable fortune" and settle down in the most magnificent house in Annapolis. Those who worked with him admired his "remarkable keenness of insight and logical power" and considered him the ablest lawyer in Maryland.

Chase and Paca became friends as law students in Annapolis and political partners at the time of the Stamp Act. They served together in the provincial assembly and on the colony's committee of correspondence, and together they attended the First and the Second Congresses. In Congress Paca let Chase serve as Maryland's mouthpiece while he gave his considerable talents to committee work. At no time did he speak on the opposite side of a question from Chase. Chase was absent from Congress the day of the vote on independence, but Paca was present. Paca on this day, a mutual friend reported to Chase, behaved "nobly and generously" which Chase knew to mean that Maryland was in the affirmative column.

John Penn
AGE: 36   LAWYER

It could have surprised few in Congress when, sometime after the Declaration had been signed, Henry Laurens of South Carolina challenged a colleague to a duel. Laurens was a rich, crusty gentleman in his mid-fifties, known for his short temper and imperious manner. The man he challenged was easy-going, amiable John Penn, "a good humored man," who "seldom spoke in Congress except it was to whisper to the member next to him." Laurens detested one of Penn's close friends, Robert Morris, whom he believed had augumented his fortune at the nation's expense. Since Morris was then out of Congress, Penn fended for him inside the chamber. During one of Penn's rare speeches from the floor, Laurens interrupted in a loud voice, singing "Poor little Penny, poor little Penny, sing tan-tarra-ra-ra." Penn overlooked the insult then but later, being a man "very talkative in company," he apparently wounded Laurens' feelings enough to provoke the challenge. The day of the duel the two men breakfasted together, for they shared the same boarding house, then set out for the field with their seconds. It was January and a street they had to cross was clogged with slush. Penn offered his arm to the older man, and after they had made the crossing he suggested they call off the duel. Laurens agreed to that, and the two men went about their business; the story, however, persisted around Philadelphia that they had "decided some nice point of honor by single combat."

Penn was born in Virginia, the son of a comfortably fixed planter who saw no reason to spend money on the education of a boy destined to be a farmer. After the father died, Edmund Pendleton, a relative and also one of Virginia's ablest lawyers and leading politicians, gave the boy the run of his large legal library. Penn was admitted to the bar when twenty-one, married two years later, and settled down in Virginia to what in the succeeding twelve years amounted to a lucrative practice. Someone persuaded him the pastures were greener in North Carolina, and on the eve of the First Congress he moved over the border into Granville County, where he had a number of relatives. The next year the county sent him to the provincial congress—possibly the post had been offered as bait to entice him into North Carolina —and after only a month's service there he went on to the Second Congress in Philadelphia.

Penn worked harmoniously in Congress with Hooper and Hewes, his colleagues from North Carolina. They agreed on all major issues. "My first wish is to be free," Hooper wrote early in February 1776; "my second is to be reconciled to Great Britain." Penn repeated the sentiment in almost identical words a week later in a letter to one of his friends. None of the three welcomed independence. "I fear most people are too sanguine" about the fruits it will bring, "especially relative to commerce," said Penn, speaking for his colleagues as well as himself, but as the pressure mounted the delegation divided. Hewes wavered, Hooper held out for reconciliation, while Penn saw independence as "a measure our enemies have forced upon us." At the end of March he returned home with Hooper to attend the provincial convention, then debating how to instruct its delegation in Congress on independence. Hooper spoke for delay; Penn called for decision. "From what I have seen there is no doubt but a total separation between Britain and her colonies, that were, will take place," he said. Leaving behind Hooper, whose health called for a holiday, Penn returned to Congress at the end of June with instructions that favored independence. He found that his friend Robert Morris, with whom he seldom disagreed, still hoped for reconciliation and could not bring himself to vote for separation from Britain. Penn nonetheless held to his decision that the time had come to break relations. Thomas Jefferson ever after believed that the conduct of North Carolina was uncertain "until Penn came, who fixed Hewes and the vote of the state."

George Ross

AGE: 46 LAWYER

There were some who thought that the remark made about his half-brother John—"Mr. John Ross, who loved ease and Madeira much better than liberty and strife, declared for neutrality, saying, that *let who would be king, he well knew that he should be subject*" —could as well have been made about George Ross. He loved his ease. Though he had "great wit, good humor, and considerable eloquence," it was said, "he possessed but little influence in Congress" because "he disliked business." He loved his Madeira. On his deathbed he remarked that he would fare well on the long journey ahead, for he was going to a cool place where "there were most excellent wines."

George Ross was born in New Castle, Delaware, the son of a clergyman who had been trained at the University of Edinburgh, decided the Presbyterians were too censorious for a man of his tastes—he, too, loved his ease and his Madeira—and shifted to the Church of England. George was still in his early years when his brother John established himself in Philadelphia, where he soon became known for an eloquence at the bar that attracted an extensive practice. With another brother Aeneas, destined for the church—Aeneas' son John later eloped with the girl who became Betsy Ross—the family's tithe to God had been paid. That left George free to read for the law in brother John's office. He was admitted to the bar when twenty years old. To escape the rough competition in Philadelphia, he moved westward to practice, opening an office in Lancaster. One of his early clients was a handsome Scotch–Irish girl; they were married within the year.

After repeal of the Stamp Act Ross "promoted a great drunken bustle" in Lancaster, but otherwise he stayed clear of politics until, at the age of thirty-eight, he won a seat in the legislature. Six years later his colleagues chose him to attend the First Congress. There he showed little enthusiasm for "the cause of Boston," and between the extreme views within his delegation—Joseph Galloway sought to conciliate the mother country while John Dickinson called for bold measures—he leaned toward Galloway.

Delegates in the Second Congress were not sure what to make of him. "Now and then he takes a whimsical turn, perhaps a wrong one," said one, attempting to explain Ross to a colleague, "but to do him justice he does not persist in it. He is too much of a *character* not to be eccentric. He is a sincere friend to the cause and I think is independent in his notions." Slowly he swung to the side of those favoring independence and for that reason was dropped from the Pennsylvania delegation late in 1775. One of the first acts of Pennsylvania's constitutional convention in July

1776 was to send him back to Congress, too late to vote for independence but in time to sign the Declaration.

Thomas Stone

AGE: 33 LAWYER

Stone preferred not to run with the pack. The ablest lawyers lived in Annapolis. Stone read for the law there in the office of Thomas Johnson, but after being admitted to the bar he moved to Frederick to practice. He married when twenty-five and proceeded to build not just a house for his wife but one of the most handsome houses in all Maryland. In 1774 he defended a poll tax to support the clergy against not only his former mentor Johnson but also Chase and Paca. The four were joined the next year when Maryland sent them as a group to the Second Congress. Stone continued to think for himself, never hesitating to oppose the boisterous Chase from the floor when he thought him wrong. At least one delegate thought Stone "was sometimes mistaken upon plain subjects." He was heard to say, for example, that "he had never known a single instance of a Negro being contented in slavery."

He did not go along with Chase's and Paca's enthusiasm for independence. "I wish to conduct affairs so that a just and honorable reconciliation should take place," he said six weeks before Virginia forced Congress to confront the question, "or that we should be pretty unanimous in a resolution to fight it out for independence. The proper way to effect this is not to move too quick. But then we must take care to do everything which is necessary for our security and defense, not suffer ourselves to be lulled or wheedled by any deceptions, declarations or givings out. You know my heart wishes for peace upon terms of security and justice to America. But war, anything, is preferable to a surrender of our rights."

By July 2 no peace commissioners had arrived from England

and Congress appeared to be "pretty unanimous" on independence. Stone voted for it.

George Taylor
AGE: 60   IRONMASTER

"He has left behind him scarce a trace by which we can discover his sentiments or actions," an early biographer reports. "He is of course almost forgotten, even in the country where he used to reside, but the old men of the neighborhood who recollect him, when asked about his character reply that 'he was a fine man and a furious Whig.' "

Taylor came from northern Ireland to Pennsylvania when twenty years old, well enough educated to become a clerk to the owner of a furnace and forge in Chester County. When the owner died he married the widow and managed the business for her. Later he and a partner leased an iron furnace in Durham, a village on the Delaware River. Tradition has it that within a few years he had "amassed a considerable fortune." When forty-seven, he relaxed his hold over the ironworks and moved his family to "a considerable estate" along the Lehigh River in Northampton County. The county sent him to the Pennsylvania Assembly, where his colleagues respected him enough to place him on several important committees. He held on to his assembly seat through five annual elections, then for some reason lost the voters' confidence. He thereupon vanished from sight for several years, but re-emerged in 1774 to lead the agitation in his county against the Boston Port Act. The county chose him colonel of a company of volunteers and sent him back to the assembly. His colleagues elected him to the committee of safety, which would direct Pennsylvania's war effort. He gave the committee little of his time and rarely attended its meetings. It was known he favored independence and when on July 20, 1776, the provincial convention voted a new slate of delegates to represent Pennsylvania in

Congress, his name was on the list, although just barely. He ran last on a ticket of eight, collecting only thirty-four votes to Franklin's seventy-eight. He showed little interest in his new assignment. Eight months after signing the Declaration he left Congress. "A respectable country gentleman," one delegate commented—he might have omitted the word "respectable" if he had known Taylor had fathered five illegitimate children by his housekeeper—"but not much distinguished in any way in Congress." Jefferson's brief tract attacking slavery, which Congress had cut from the Declaration, made no impression upon him; he died owning two slaves.

George Walton

AGE: ABOUT 35   LAWYER

The records say he was born in 1741, but somehow Benjamin Rush got the idea Walton "was the youngest member of Congress, being not quite three and twenty when he signed the Declaration of Independence." The error is puzzling, for the two men were particular friends. They shared the same political views, being early and fervent supporters of independence. They saw each other often in Philadelphia, and Rush, who rarely presumed with those he did not know well, did not hesitate to borrow Walton's carriage when his own was not handy. After returning to Georgia, Walton wrote that he was collecting his papers and sending them up to Philadelphia for safe keeping with his good friend Rush.

But the records say that Walton was thirty-five when he signed the Declaration, that he was born in Virginia, and left an orphan when still a child. An uncle reared him until he was old enough to be apprenticed to a carpenter. Walton, it is recorded, impressed his master as a young man suited for something better than the hammer and saw. The carpenter tore up the apprentice contract and sent the boy off to do as he wished with his life. He surfaced next in Georgia, where in 1774 at the age of thirty-three (or twenty-one by Rush's calculation) he was admitted to the bar. In the same year he joined the local committee of correspondence. Except for the parish of St. John along the coast, inhabited largely by transplanted New Englanders, Georgia leaned toward loyalty to the mother country, but Walton had brought with him all the enthusiasm for resistance then being displayed in his native Virginia. In 1775 he helped organize the provincial congress, which elected him its secretary. That same year he married—happily it appeared; he always addressed his wife as "my dear girl" or "my dear Polly" and once wrote, "God bless you, my dear, and remember you are sincerely loved by a man who wishes to make honor and reputation the rule of all his actions." And 1775 also saw him chosen president of the newly created council of safety. He was sent to Congress early in 1776.

Walton impressed his new colleagues at once. He was a small man, no taller than the diminutive Hopkinson, but there the resemblance stopped, for Walton was haughty in demeanor and plagued with a violent temper. Nor was he "very abstemious in his manner of living," according to a contemporary, "and his partiality for study imparted a sedentary habit at an early period of life; hence, before he attained its meridian, he was afflicted with gout, which caused him much suffering during his declining years." He hated Button Gwinnett and either because of "different principles or different judgments" often did not vote as Hall did, except on the question of independence, for which both were zealous supporters. He spoke well and to the point when he took the floor. He handled committee assignments deftly and with dispatch. He differed from fellow Southerners in that he favored a strong central government for America, and it may have been this that carried him into a friendship with Robert Morris. Later, when Congress retreated to Baltimore, Walton stayed behind in Philadelphia, at the risk of capture by the British, and teamed up with George Clymer and Morris—they made an incongruous trio, the diminutive backwoods lawyer from Georgia flanked by the two imposing Philadelphia merchants—to create an informal war office that performed so efficiently that both Congress and Washington were impressed.

For his friend Rush he exemplified the spirit of '76. After signing the Declaration, he returned home to fill "the offices of governor and chief justice for many years in Georgia, and evinced in his public conduct the same attachment to government and order, that he had done in 1776 to liberty and independence."

$\mathscr{G}$eorge $\mathscr{W}$ythe

AGE: 50   LAWYER

"The following account of Mr. Wythe is much less circumstantial than is required by the dignity of the subject," an early biographer wrote. "Of his private and domestic transactions, he has left himself no remembrance, and his friends, by whose aid we hoped to supply the deficiency, appear to have postponed this principal object, to indulge in expressions of affection for his memory, and have furnished us rather a panegyric than a history of his life." Among those included in this gentle reprimand were Thomas Jefferson, John Marshall, and Henry Clay, all former students of Wythe's. But even with those who knew him less well Wythe inspired praise. "A profound lawyer and able politician," said a colleague who knew him in Congress. "He seldom spoke in Congress, but when he did his speeches were sensible, correct, and pertinent. I have seldom known a man possess more modesty, or a more dove-like simplicity and gentleness of manner."

Wythe appeared to be Parson Weems' kind of man, cut from the mold that had shaped Washington, but "having been often told that though the *honestest* man in Virginia," he "was not the most orthodox," Weems went out of his way to "learn his real sentiments about religion." Wythe invited Weems to dinner. "Being altogether granivorous [one who feeds on grain] himself, he gave me a dinner exactly to his own tooth; *rice* milk improved with plums, sugar and nutmeg," said Weems. While consuming "this demulcent diet" Wythe agreed that religion is "our *best* and *greatest* friend," that it furnished "the best of all motives to virtue; the strongest dissuasives to vice." Christianity, of all religions, is "the *sweetest* and *sublimest* in the world," for it "labors throughout to infix in our hearts this great truth, that God is love," he concluded, having satisfied Weems without committing himself to church-going or any particular sect.

Virginians regarded Wythe as their greatest legal scholar, and the pedantic phrases for which he had a weakness kept them reminded of his erudition. His reverence for the law led one man to wonder whether he was a fool or a saint, a confusion provoked by a letter he had received from Wythe:

Sir:
The suit wherein you were pleased to do me the honor to engage my services, was last week brought to trial, and has fully satisfied me that you were entirely in the wrong. Knowing you to be a perfectly honest man, I concluded that you have somehow or other been misled. At any rate, I find that I have been altogether misled in the affair, and therefore insist on washing my hands of it immediately.

Thereafter, when Wythe had doubts about a client he "required the solemnity of an oath previous to his defense, and if deception was in any manner practiced upon him, the fee was returned and the cause abandoned." He had another peculiarity—he took the words "liberty" and "freedom" with embarrassing literalness, applying them to black men as well as white, and freed his slaves upon his death. (Only he and Washington among the revolutionary leaders of Virginia did so. Wythe, unlike Washington, "did not cast them on the world friendless and needy," but willed them a share of his estate in trust.)

The need to earn a living as much as an inclination for scholarship sent Wythe into law. When he was three his father died, leaving the family plantation to his older brother. His mother, who gave him a grounding in Latin and Greek, died a few years later. A relative allowed him to read law in his office, and at the age of twenty Wythe was admitted to the bar. He began to practice with an attorney in the frontier county of Spotsylvania. He married his partner's sister, only to have her die the next year. The next seven years passed quietly as he built a practice and a reputation. His luck changed in his twenty-seventh year when he was elected to the House of Burgesses and simultaneously chosen by the governor to serve as acting attorney general while Edmund Pendleton, who normally filled the office, was in England. (Wythe and Pendleton had been courtroom rivals for years, with Wythe's lucid but dry presentations to juries usually losing out to Pendleton's more dramatic style. After one defeat Wythe in despair said he was going home, give up the law, take orders and preach the gospel. "Yes," said a friend, "and then Pendleton will go home, give up the law, take orders, preach the gospel, and beat you there.")

Soon after he became acting attorney general Wythe's brother died and the family estate descended to him. A short while later he married again and settled permanently in Williamsburg, leaving others to manage his plantation. In Williamsburg he built a considerable practice, read to his heart's content in the law and classics, and saw much of the cultivated governor, Francis Fauquier, and also William and Mary's professor of natural philosophy, William Small, who introduced him to a favorite student, Thomas Jefferson. The four gentlemen often spent evenings together in "philosophic conversation."

Wythe's opposition to the mother country began with the Stamp Act and owed much to his reverence for the law. The new imperial policy was wrong because it was illegal. The past, as he read it, showed Parliament had no authority over the colonies and the colonies' only tie with Britain was through the crown. He preached this gospel for the next ten years, making few converts except young Jefferson, but when the times caught up with his views, Virginia sent him to the Second Congress. There, for all his "dove-like simplicity," he emerged as a quiet but adroit promoter of independence. Samuel Adams called him a "much valued friend." Five months before independence Wythe in one of his rare speeches in Congress said the delegates had the right to make foreign alliances, like the representatives of any other nation. "An objection being offered that this was independence," a member reported, "there ensued much argument upon that ground." Late in March 1776 Wythe tacked on to the tail of an innocent proposal dealing with privateers an amendment "wherein the king was made the author of our miseries instead of the ministry." Again those for reconciliation argued, quite rightly, "that this was effectually severing the king from us forever," as Wythe well knew. When Thomas Nelson arrived from Virginia with the resolution that directed Congress to face the question of independence, Wythe saw his work in Philadelphia done, for the moment at least. Virginia was preparing to create a constitution. Now that independence was inevitable, he must put his mind on the kind of government Virginia should have. Wythe, with Richard Henry Lee, left Congress in June before the resolution for independence came up for a vote. He signed the embossed copy of the Declaration when he returned to Congress in September 1776.

Few of these men thought themselves in the midst of a revolution when they came to the Second Continental Congress. Indeed, most saw themselves engaged in a civil war— Englishmen against Englishmen, and worse, Americans against Americans. "The son is armed against the father," one man said, "the brother against the brother, family against family." William Hooper's family split down the middle. Francis Lewis' daughter married a British officer, and he ceased to speak to her. Caesar Rodney lost his friend William Allen to the Loyalist cause, and Benjamin Franklin his son William and his political ally of many years, Joseph Galloway. Only slowly did the word "revolution" supplant that of "civil war" in the delegates' letters, and even then it was used to mean only "improvement without metamorphosis."

The question of independence came upon the delegates

with startling suddenness, and each of the men who eventually signed the Declaration of Independence approached his decision by a private route. Each moved cautiously, aware that "the eyes of the world" were upon Congress. Most, as they edged toward a pledge of their lives, their fortunes, and their sacred honor, felt themselves to be what they have aptly been called—"reluctant rebels."

8

The Penman

Congress resolved on June 11: "That the Committee to prepare a declaration consist of five members. The members chosen, Mr. Jefferson, Mr. J. Adams, Mr. Franklin, Mr. Sherman, and Mr. Livingston." All sections of the country were represented—the South (Jefferson), New England (Adams and Sherman), and the Middle Colonies (Franklin and Livingston)—and one member of Congress who had opposed independence (Livingston) had been put on the committee to assure those for postponement that while separation from Great Britain might be inevitable, the document that would declare it to the world would contain nothing to offend the more conservative delegates.

The committee of five convened within a day or two of its appointment, but it met as a committee of four. Benjamin Franklin stayed away; he was suffering from an attack of the gout. He spent most of June on a friend's farm outside the city.

When the committee met, all knew Jefferson would serve

as chairman. He had received the most votes, he was admired for his skill as a writer, and since Virginia had forced the resolution for independence on Congress a Virginian was naturally expected to write the document that would declare the news to the world.

Thomas Jefferson
AGE: 33   LAWYER

Mr. Jefferson as seen by one of his overseers:

Mr. Jefferson was six feet two and a half inches high, well proportioned, and straight as a gun-barrel. He was like a fine horse —he had no surplus flesh. He had an iron constitution, and was very strong. He had a machine for measuring strength. There were very few men that I have seen try it, that were as strong in the arms as his son-in-law Col. Thomas Mann Randolph; but Mr. Jefferson was stronger than he. He always enjoyed the best of health. His skin was very clear and pure—just like he was in principle. He had blue eyes. His countenance was always mild and pleasant. You never saw it ruffled. No odds what happened, it always maintained the same expression. When I was sometimes very much fretted and disturbed, his countenance was perfectly unmoved. I remember one case in particular. We had about eleven thousand bushels of wheat in the mill, and coopers and everything else employed. There was a big freshet—the first after the dam was finished. It was raining powerfully. I got up early in the morning, and went up to the dam. While I stood there, it began to break, and I stood and saw the freshet sweep it all away. I never felt worse. I did not know what we should do. I went up to see Mr. Jefferson. He had just come from breakfast.

"Well, sir," said he, "have you heard from the river?"

I said: "Yes, sir; I have just come from there with very bad news. The mill dam is all swept away."

"Well, sir," said he, just as calm and quiet as though nothing had happened, "we can't make a new dam this summer, but we will get Lewis' ferry-boat, with our own, and get the hands from all the quarters, and boat in rock enough in place of the dam, to answer for the present and next summer. I will send to Baltimore and get ship-bolts, and we will make a dam that the freshet can't wash away."

He then went on and explained to me in detail just how he would have the dam built. We repaired the dam as he suggested, and the next summer we made a new dam, that I reckon must be there yet.

Mr. Jefferson was always an early riser—arose at daybreak, or before. The sun never found him in bed. I used sometimes to think, when I went up there *very* early in the morning, that I would find him in bed; but there he would be before me, walking on the terrace.

He never had a servant make a fire in his room in the morning, or at any other time, when he was at home. He always had a box filled with nice dry wood in his room, and when he wanted fire he would open it and put on the wood. He would always have a good many ashes in his fireplace, and when he went out he would cover up his fire very carefully, and when he came back he would uncover the coals and make a fire for himself.

He did not use tobacco in any form. He never used a profane word or anything like it. He never played cards. I never saw a card in the house at Monticello, and I had particular orders from him to suppress card-playing among the Negroes, who, you know, are generally very fond of it. I never saw any dancing in his house, and if there had been any there during the twenty years I was with him I should certainly have known it. He was never a great eater, but what he did eat he wanted to be very choice. He never eat much hog-meat. He often told me, as I was giving out meat for the servants, that what I gave one of them for a week would be more than he would use in six months.

When he was coming home I generally knew it, and got ready for him, and waited at the house to give him the keys. After saying "How are all?" and talking awhile, he would say, "What have you got that is good?" I knew mighty well what suited him. He was especially fond of Guinea fowls; and for meat he preferred good beef, mutton, and lambs. He was very fond of vegetables and fruit, and raised every variety of them. He was very ingenious. He invented a plough that was considered a great improvement on any that had ever been used. He got a great many premiums and medals for it. He planned his own carriage, buildings, gárden, fences, and a good many other things. He was nearly always busy upon some plan or model.

Every day, most as regularly as the day came, unless the weather was very bad, he would have his horse brought out and take his ride. The boy who took care of his horse knew what time he started, and would bring him out for him, and hitch him in his place. He generally started about nine o'clock. He was an uncommonly fine rider—sat easily upon his horse, and always had him in the most perfect control.

He was always very neat in his dress, wore short breeches and bright shoe buckles. When he rode on horseback he had a pair of overalls that he always put on.

Mr. Jefferson never debarred himself from hearing any preacher that came along. There was a Mr. Hiter, a Baptist preacher, that used to preach occasionally at the Charlottesville Court House. He had no regular church, but was a kind of missionary—rode all over the country and preached. He wasn't much of a preacher, was uneducated, but he was a good man. Everybody had confidence in him, and they went to hear him on that account. Mr. Jefferson nearly always went to hear him when he came around. I remember his being there one day in particular. His servant came with him and brought a seat—a kind of camp stool, upon which he sat. After the sermon there was a proposition to pass round the hat and raise money to buy the preacher a horse. Mr. Jefferson did not wait for the hat. I saw him unbutton his overalls, and get his hand into his pocket, and take out a handful of silver, I don't know how much. He then walked across the Court House to Mr. Hiter, and gave it into his hand. He bowed very politely to Mr. Jefferson, and seemed to be very much pleased.

At the first meeting of the committee of five Jefferson suggested, as a courteous gentleman, that Adams, who had worked harder and longer for separation, should write the Declaration.

"I will not," said Adams.
"You should do it," Jefferson said.
"Oh, no."
"Why will you not?" asked Jefferson. "You ought to do it."
"I will not."
"Why?"
"Reasons enough."
"What can be your reasons?" Jefferson insisted.
"Reason first—You are a Virginian, and a Virginian ought to

appear at the head of this business. Reason second—I am obnoxious, suspected, and unpopular. You are very much otherwise. Reason third—You can write ten times better than I can."

"Well," said Jefferson, "if you are decided, I will do as well as I can."

"Very well," said Adams. "When you have drawn it up, we will have a meeting."

This gracious exchange took some effort on Adams' part. He was at the time more distinguished than Jefferson and eight years his senior. However, relinquishing the chance to write the document he had for so many months urged on Congress came easier because he both admired and liked Jefferson. He later recalled that the Virginian had soon impressed him upon arriving in Philadelphia in 1775 as "prompt, frank, explicit, and decisive upon committees and in conversation," so much so "that he soon seized upon my heart." The judgment is all the more remarkable because the two men outwardly held so little in common. Jefferson towered more than a half foot above the stubby Adams. He was a rich man who spent money easily; Adams owned a modest farm and the small income it gave him led to constant worry about money. Jefferson had traveled to Philadelphia with four horses and two slaves as servants; Adams traveled from Massachusetts astride his horse. Adams lived in a boardinghouse, but Jefferson, to escape the heat of the city, had taken a small apartment on the outskirts of town.

Jefferson had been reared in a world strange to John Adams. At the age of fourteen Jefferson had inherited from his father, who had recently died, twenty-seven hundred acres of land, sixty slaves, twenty-five horses, two hundred hogs, and seventy head of cattle—in short, a plantation which, transplanted to Massachusetts, would have made him one of the colony's richest landowners. When he was sixteen, he left the plantation to overseers to run and traveled from his home in the back country down to Williamsburg, the colony's capital, to attend William and Mary College. There he built on the foundation of Latin, Greek, and French acquired from a clergyman who had tutored him and won the reputation he would win again in Congress, of being a great "rubber off of dust." Then, as all through life, he rose with the sun, worked an hour or two before breakfast, and continued to work through the day. Often in the twilight he jogged a mile or so out into the countryside to clear the brain for an evening of further study. It is hard to accept his later confession that he fell into "bad company" in college and that he remained forever astonished he "did not turn off with some of them, and become as worthless to society as they were."

Jefferson left college after two years but remained in Williamsburg to read law with George Wythe, Virginia's most distinguished legal mind. Wythe introduced him to Governor Francis Fauquier. Jefferson said that during the evenings he spent in the Palace, as the governor's mansion was called, he "heard more good sense, more rational and philosophic conversation, than in all my life besides." There was music, too, for the governor was fond of it, and when he learned that Jefferson played the violin, he "associated [him] with two or three other amateurs in his weekly concerts."

Under Wythe's guidance, Jefferson continued his dawn to past-dark reading schedule. He read in philosophy, science, and religion, as well as law, and found time for poetry and novels, for "everything is useful which contributes to fix us in the principles of virtue." He always read to a purpose. The Greek and Latin authors taught him that a man born to wealth had a duty to serve the people and that a man who pursued happiness found it only by living moderately, reasonably, and virtuously.

The year of the Stamp Act, when John Adams first immersed himself in politics, Jefferson also lifted his head out of his books. He was on hand when Patrick Henry rose in the House of Burgesses to denounce the Stamp Act, and for years afterward could recall the "torrents of sublime eloquence from Mr. Henry" and that the debate that afternoon had been "most bloody." The next year he traveled up to Philadelphia to be inoculated against smallpox, an act that suited his cautiously bold character; many of the day viewed inoculation with live smallpox germs a needless risk, except when an epidemic was upon them. He was admitted to the Virginia bar the following year. After practicing for two years his name and face were known throughout the county. He ran for the House of Burgesses, was elected, and took his seat in early May 1769. He prepared for the new career in the same thorough way he did everything—by buying a small library of books on government.

Shortly before his twenty-ninth birthday Jefferson married a wealthy widow, whose estate joined to his made him one of the largest landowners in Virginia. The house to which he carried his bride sat on a mountaintop. He called it Monticello, an Italian word meaning "little mountain," and upon it he would lavish all the thought and energy he gave to any project he undertook. "They was forty years at work on that house before Mr. Jefferson stopped building," one of his slaves said.

In 1774 Jefferson had served six years in the House but had not achieved enough stature to be sent to the First Continental Congress that convened that autumn. Back at Monticello he wrote a pamphlet which came out under the title *A Summary View of the Rights of British America*. It was an incredibly bold—brash even —attack against George III. If the king expects things to settle down in America, said Jefferson, he would do well to mend his ways. He has many sins to account for. He has delayed consideration of our laws; endeavored to take from the people the right of representation; dissolved representative bodies doing their duty; delayed the issue of writs for choice of new representatives; perpetuated feudal landholding practices; and sent troops among us. Jefferson dared even to accuse the king of forcing slavery upon the colonies, an evil which insults "the rights of human nature." He ended the essay with some impudent advice from a young man to his monarch: "The whole art of government consists in the art of being honest. Only aim to do your duty, and mankind will give you credit where you fail."

The pamphlet made Jefferson famous overnight, and led the Virginia convention—the governor had refused to let the legislature meet and so the members convened informally and illegally in a convention—to send him to the Second Congress in May of 1775. The delegates in Philadelphia studied the young man who had dared insult the king with care. He wore "a loose, shackling air" about him, it was observed, "a rambling vacant look" and ambled along at an "easy and swinging" pace. He had long arms and legs, large wrists, a jutting chin, light red hair, and a brick-colored face. A slave of his called him "as neat a built man as ever was seen in Vaginny, I reckon, or any place—a straight-up man, long face, high nose," but others less generous likened him to "a tall large-boned farmer." He almost never spoke from the floor of Congress and away from Congress rarely talked about himself, always turning the conversation "to subjects most familiar to those with whom he conversed, whether laborer, mechanic, or other." He impressed his colleagues as a solid, able delegate. Few noticed that "it constituted a part of Mr. Jefferson's pride," as a friend remarked, "to run before the times in which he lived."

Jefferson attended Congress irregularly. His wife's constant ill-health kept him in a suspense "too terrible to be endured" and drew him often home to Monticello. The early months of 1776 found him in Virginia, leaving it to others to prod Congress to declare independence. Not until mid-May did he return to Phila-delphia. Even then he came reluctantly; he wanted to be in Virginia, where the convention was about to draw up a constitu-tion for the colony. "It is work of the most interesting nature and such as every individual would wish to have his voice in," he said. "In truth, it is the whole subject of the present controversy."

He resumed his seat in Congress on May 14 but gave little time to the campaign for independence. Instead, he worked on a con-stitution for Virginia. His draft opened with a long list of the king's wrongs; these justified Virginia creating a constitution for itself. Jefferson then went on to advance a number of innovations for the new government. He thought the right to vote should be extended to virtually all white adult males in the colony. "Who-ever intends to live in a country must wish that country well," he said, "and has a natural right of assisting in the preservation of it." He wanted to end the established, that is, the state-supported and protected, church and allow "all persons" to "have full and free liberty of religious opinion." In a day when a man who stole a silver spoon risked death by hanging he dared to call for an end to all capital punishment except for the crime of murder. He also wanted to end slavery and inserted a clause in his draft that said "no person hereafter coming into this country shall be held in slavery under any pretext whatever."

Jefferson did all he could to get recalled to Virginia in order to present his draft to the constitutional convention, but he knew that the long-postponed vacation due to Richard Henry Lee and George Wythe meant he must stay in Philadelphia. Thus, against his own desire, he found himself in Congress on June 11 when the delegates chose him to head the committee created to draw up the Declaration of Independence.

Six months earlier Thomas Paine in *Common Sense* had defined the task that Congress had handed Jefferson. He urged that a manifesto "be published and dispatched to foreign courts, setting forth the miseries we have endured and the peaceful methods which we have ineffectually used for redress." This manifesto should declare to the world "that not being able any longer to live happily or safely under the cruel disposition of the British court, we had been driven to the necessity of breaking off all connections with her." Since the monarchs of Europe were bound to be suspicious of colonies rebelling against one of their brethren, the document should assure "all such courts of our peaceable disposition towards them, and of our desire of entering into trade with them." Such a document, Paine concluded, "would produce more good effects to this continent than if a ship were freighted with petitions to Britain."

Consciously or not, Jefferson followed Paine's suggestions when he began the Declaration of Independence as if they were orders. He knew his manifesto must appeal to the American people as well as foreign courts, but like Paine he also knew that the main job of the paper was to convince the world that what America was doing was right, that she "had been driven to the necessity" of breaking away from Great Britain.

Jefferson wrote his paper in the quiet of the second-floor apartment he had moved to in order to escape "the excessive heats of the city" and to "have the benefit of a freely circulating air." He worked at a portable desk light enough to rest comfortably on his knees. He wrote quickly, probably taking no more than a morning to complete the first draft. He began with a statement of purpose, which would be substantially revised before the world saw it:

When in the course of human events it becomes necessary for a people to advance from that subordination in which they have hitherto remained, & to assume among the powers of the earth the equal & independant station to which the laws of nature & of nature's god entitled them, a decent respect to the opinions of mankind requires that they should declare the causes which impel them to the change.

No one in Congress except John Adams had read more widely in political literature than Jefferson, but in his opening lines he made clear he would draw principally, for his argument, from a book all the delegates were familiar with—John Locke's *Two Treatises of Government.* In that book Locke developed a justification for the "right of rebellion." Men were born free, in a state of nature and unhampered by government. The laws of nature endowed them with certain "self-evident" natural rights, among which were the rights to life, liberty, and property. Now, the state of nature is difficult to maintain, for evil exists in the world and there are times when a man alone cannot cope with it. To protect their rights, men voluntarily band together and make a compact or agreement whereby one of their own is chosen to rule over them. This ruler, with the people's consent, creates a government whose sole purpose is to protect men's natural rights. If the ruler fails to protect these rights, fails to carry out his duties, the people have the right to rebel, for their ruler has broken the original compact they made with him. But before they rebel, they must tell the world "the causes which impel them to the change."

Jefferson's next sentence, which would also be much rewritten, develops these ideas of Locke:

We hold these truths to be sacred and undeniable; that all men are created equal & independant, that from that equal creation they derive rights inherent & inalienable, among which are the preservation of life, & liberty & the pursuit of happiness.

But here Jefferson made a major change. From Locke's trio of natural rights—life, liberty, and property—he dropped the last and added a new one. He did this with reason. His manifesto must appeal to all Americans, and many who were fighting to win America's freedom owned little or no property. The words he substituted for property—the pursuit of happiness—were borrowed from a friend who had written of man's right of "pursuing and obtaining happiness." Jefferson changed the wording, because he knew that while man had a right to pursue happiness he did not necessarily have a right to obtain it.

The theoretical basis for revolt had been laid down. Jefferson now moved on to submit "facts to a candid world," or as Paine put it, to set "forth the miseries we have endured" that justified the American revolt. He did not have to rummage through his mind to collect these facts. The list of charges against the king he had drawn up as a preface for his draft of a constitution for Virginia were slipped in here. But in copying over the list Jefferson dreamed up several new charges, one of them a lengthy paragraph that blamed the imposition of slavery upon America on the king. George III, said Jefferson, has "determined to keep open a market where MEN should be bought and sold, he has prostituted his negative for suppressing every legislative attempt to prohibit or to restrain this execrable commerce."

Some, upon first meeting Jefferson, found him a cool gentleman—"nay, even cold," said one—but nothing in the concluding paragraphs of his manifesto reveals this side of his character. He writes with almost unrestrained passion. "These facts have given the last stab to agonizing affection and manly spirit bids us to renounce forever these unfeeling brethren," goes one sentence. Some of his most vivid phrases now come forth: Our former brethren we must now hold "as we hold the rest of mankind, enemies in war, in peace friends." We must now climb alone "the road to happiness and to glory." From these lines he moves to a formal renouncement of all ties to Great Britain, and then ends with one of the great sentences in the English language:

And for the support of this declaration we mutually pledge to each other our lives, our fortunes, & our sacred honour.

With the first draft completed, Jefferson began tinkering with his handiwork, cutting out a word here, adding one there. He decided, for example, that it sounded better to say "We hold these truths to be self-evident," rather than that they were "sacred & undeniable." The polishing done, he showed the document to John Adams, who liked it so much that he took time to make his own copy.

Between the time Adams returned the draft to Jefferson and when it was laid before Congress some thirty-one changes were made in the paper by Jefferson and members of the committee. The first two sentences were polished to their final form, and three new charges against the king were added. All other changes were minor. Everyone seemed highly satisfied with what Jefferson had done.

And exactly what had he done? He had, most skillfully, courted sympathy abroad. The eloquent but restrained opening passages, followed by the long list of the king's abuses of his power, revealed that the American people were acting only after endless suffering. Jefferson had carefully avoided attacking the monarchical form of government—to do so would have angered all the crowned heads of Europe—and centered his blast on a single misguided king, George III. No hint of praise for a republican government appeared in the document. Americans were made to appear not as rebels but as a long-suffering, much put upon people who with great reluctance were breaking away from their mother country because of an evil monarch who had attempted to corrupt their way of life.

Jefferson managed at the same time he appealed to Europe to promote unity at home. The catalogue of George III's transgressions touched on every section of the country. Few colonists could read the list without feeling that somewhere along the line they had been directly injured by the king. This was a remarkable achievement, considering the splits that had divided Congress the past several months. There was little in the paper, except possibly the indictment against slavery, likely to irritate any delegate, regardless of what part of the continent he came from.

As if this were not enough, Jefferson did more. In announcing America's independence, he made the new nation appear as a land of promise. We will climb "the road to happiness & glory," he said. We are a virtuous people and whatever corruption exists among us was imposed on us by Great Britain. Separation, he implied, would bring much more than a change of masters. Exactly what it would bring was unclear, but no hint of doubt that great changes were in the making turns up in the paper. By the substitution of the phrase "pursuit of happiness" for the word "property," Jefferson made America seem a place where human rights ranked above all others, especially the rights of property.

For all its virtues, Jefferson's paper had a major flaw. He had simplified the highly complex issues dividing the colonies from Britain into a drama of good versus evil. It was, perhaps, hardly possible in a short paper appealing to world opinion for Jefferson to have done otherwise, but the result of this approach would be unfortunate in the long run. All the arguments in the great debate in Congress early in June had centered on what was best for America, what would do the most to promote the colonies' own interests. By obscuring the role of self-interest in shaping the decision on independence, Jefferson's paper propagated an unrealistic picture of how and why political decisions are made. But before the paper was given to the world Congress must approve it. Perhaps the delegates would edit Jefferson's paper in a way that would alleviate its single flaw.

9

July 1

Before Jefferson's paper could be dealt with, the question of independence itself still had to be settled, and this, on Monday, July 1, Congress proceeded to do. Much had occurred in the three weeks that had elapsed since Congress had formally discussed the issue. In Pennsylvania a provincial conference had usurped power from the official legislature, then announced its "willingness to concur in a vote of the Congress declaring the United Colonies free and independent states." The assembly of Delaware had set about creating a new government, free of royal authority, and by implication had given its delegates in Congress a free hand on the question of independence. Caesar Rodney was still absent and trying to speed the transition in Delaware's political affairs when Congress assembled in the morning heat of July 1. New Jersey had ejected Governor William Franklin, who, to his father's distress, chose to remain loyal to Great Britain. It had also elected a new slate of delegates to represent it in Congress. The delegation appeared for the first time on July 1. Nothing revealed more clearly the chaotic state of New Jersey politics at that moment than the five men it had sent to Congress—a disparate collection of misfits and gadflies, topped off by an unassuming farmer and a lighthearted man of good humor who had no business being in politics.

Richard Stockton
AGE: 45   LAWYER

He was wealthy. He stood nearly six feet tall and had a commanding presence. He was a superb horseman and skilled in the use of the sword. Only a "somewhat hasty" temper marred his character. He lived in baronial splendor at Morven Manor on the edge of Princeton, with a handsome wife whom he addressed as "my dearest love" and six engaging children, the eldest of whom his fellow Signer, Benjamin Rush, married.

Stockton and his wife had made the spacious garden at Morven, patterned on Alexander Pope's garden at Twickenham, one of the loveliest in America. He moved sedately through life insulated from politics. "The public is generally unthankful," he said, "and I never will become a servant of it till I am convinced that by neglecting my own affairs I am doing more acceptable service to God and man." He should never have accepted his seat in Congress. None signed the Declaration, not even the doubters, more confused than he, more torn between attachment to England and affection for America. "He was timid where bold measures were required," said his son-in-law, and timidity—or unresolved doubts—contributed to his humiliation a few months after casting a vote for independence.

Stockton's father—lawyer, judge, devout Presbyterian— trained his son to follow in his steps. A clergyman gave the boy a sound grounding in religion and the three R's. Stockton moved on to the Presbyterian College of New Jersey—located at the time in Newark but later in Princeton where the Stocktons, chief among its shepherds, could keep a close eye on its affairs—and then read for the law. Admission to the bar came when he was twenty-four, and he prospered at once. His reputation swelled so great "that the first gentlemen of the country," said a loquacious contemporary, "considered it of material importance to the future prospects of their sons to procure their instruction in the science of law under the inspection of Mr. Stockton."

Stockton opposed the Stamp Act, but decorously, and two years later when in London on business was still enough in favor to be received by the king and the king's chief minister, the Marquis of Rockingham. After a side trip to Scotland to offer the presidency of the College of New Jersey to John Witherspoon, Stockton returned home to become, without enduring the rough and tumble of an election, a man of political importance. Governor William Franklin appointed him to the provincial council, a post he held until the end of royal government in the colony. Six years later he accepted a seat on the supreme court.

As a judge Stockton revered the British constitution; as a lawyer he reviled the likes of Abraham Clark, who denounced the high cost of justice in time and legal fees. Stockton's firm stand during an outburst in New Jersey against lawyers, possibly inspired by Clark, kept the courts open. "He loved law and order," said his son-in-law, "and once offended his constituents by opposing the seizure of private property in an illegal manner by an officer of the army."

The increasing animosity toward Britain after the First Congress adjourned convinced Stockton that unless a compromise were soon reached an "obstinate, awful, and tremendous war" would break forth. His own solution, which he sent to one of the king's ministers, called for granting "self-government for America, independent of Parliament, without renouncing allegiance to the crown." He had still not made up his mind about independence when elected to the Second Congress on June 22, 1776. "Judge Stockton was most particularly importunate" to hear all the arguments, for and against, the day he took his seat.

He was obliged and the next day voted for independence. He may have been swayed to throw in his lot with the Revolution by the supposed certainty he would soon "take charge of the government of New Jersey, an event which all parties say is inevitable." It was not inevitable. After a tie vote for governor in the New Jersey legislature, William Livingston won on the next ballot by a majority of one, and Stockton had to be satisfied with the post of chief justice of the newly created supreme court.

Four months after he had signed the Declaration, the British commandeered Stockton's estate in Princeton for their headquarters. He fled to the house of a friend. A relative informed the British of his whereabouts. He was taken prisoner, and after a tortuous trip over icy roads thrown in jail. There, Congress heard, he "suffers many indignities and hardships from the enemy, from which not only his rank, but his being a man, ought to exempt him." Congress protested his treatment, but too late. The torment had broken his spirit. Shortly before he was released he signed a pledge to "remain in a peaceful obedience to his Majesty and not take up arms, nor encourage others to take up arms, in opposition to his authority." He returned to Princeton to find his house looted. Among the townspeople who had regarded him as the first citizen of Princeton he was "much spoke against for his conduct."

John Witherspoon
AGE: 53   CLERGYMAN

Congress could tolerate any number of ministers' sons in its midst. It could even put up with the piety of a Samuel Adams or a Roger Sherman. It found it hard, though, to accept a true ecclesiastic. Earlier it had endured the learned John Joachim Zubly, a Presbyterian clergyman from Georgia. Zubly departed *"abruptly"* from his colleagues in November 1775 "because they would not come into his plan of *petitioning* again, and because he was against independency, which he plainly saw the Congress had resolved on." Then on July 1, 1776, came John Witherspoon, another learned Presbyterian clergyman and just as rigid as Zubly. He happened, however, to be a zealot for independence.

Witherspoon arrived with impressive credentials. In Scotland, he had achieved fame as a witty, persuasive opponent of those within the church who wished to dilute traditional Presbyterian doctrines. He would have no tampering with the belief in predestination nor countenance such devilish forms of recreation as dancing, card playing, or the theater. Richard Stockton, helped by Benjamin Rush—"a most agreeable young man," said Witherspoon, though addicted to "strong and superlative expressions"—brought him to America as president of the College of New Jersey in Princeton. While remaking the school—he enlarged the endowment, strengthened the faculty, broadened the curriculum, and by attracting boys from outside New Jersey gave it something of a continental reputation—he used his prestige to start healing the breach between Old Side and New Side Presbyterians which had divided the church in America for nearly a generation.

He brought more than his prestige as a churchman to Congress. He was a tall man and radiated "more of the quality of *presence*" than any man in America except George Washington, so it was said. He excelled as an orator, being "remarkably luminous and correct in all his speeches," and so dextrous in argument that he would "astonish the whole house by the regular arrangement of his ideas, his command of language, and his precision on subjects of importance." He spoke without notes, in a low voice with a heavy Scotch accent one delegate called "mitten-muffled," and always kept a tight rein on his emotions. (A friend explained why: "A peculiar affection of the nerves, attended with dizziness, which always overcame him when he gave free vent to his feelings on any subject, obliged him, from his earliest entrance on public life, to impose a strict restraint and guard upon his sensibility; he once, indeed, fell from the pulpit in a moment of irresistible religious excitation.") Above all, he was a superb politician, or as one delegate put it, had "all the design and arch cunning that is necessary or practiced in an assembly of the kirk in Scotland."

Witherspoon would remain in Congress for six years and serve on more than one hundred committees. Yet his colleagues never embraced him with enthusiasm. "His influence was less than might have been expected from his abilities and knowledge," one said, "owing in part to his ecclesiastical character." But even if he had arrived wearing no frock the delegates would have continued to hold him at a distance. He was a hard man—a "sordid and arbitrary" Scotsman, a sometime friend once called him—and could be unforgiving to those who crossed him. He hated Thomas Paine, and when someone nominated the author for the post of secretary to the newly created committee for foreign affairs, Witherspoon objected strenuously. He said that when Paine first came to America he had favored reconciliation but upon "finding the tide of popularity run rapidly, he had turned about; that he was very intemperate and could not write until he had quickened his thoughts with large draughts of rum and water; that he was, in short, a bad character, and not fit to be placed in such a situation." Congress ignored the objections and gave Paine the job. ("Parsons were always mischievous fellows when they turned politicians," said Paine.)

When the roll call reached New Jersey and it came time for Witherspoon to cast his vote on July 2, he rose to give a short sermon with his "aye." The continent "had been for some time past loud in its demand for the proposed declaration," he admonished his colleagues; in fact, "it was not only ripe for the measure but in danger of rotting for the want of it." The British quickly made him pay for his brashness. "Old Weatherspoon has not escaped their fury," a colleague reported five months after the signing of the Declaration. "They have burnt his library. It grieves him much that he has lost his controversial tracts. He would lay aside the cloth to take revenge on them. I believe he would send them to the Devil if he could."

Abraham Clark

AGE: 50   POLITICIAN

He bubbled with suspicion—of other men's motives, of unchecked power, of strong government, of hereditary privileges, of lawyers, of any attempt to infringe upon the rights of New Jersey. "A sensible but cynical man," said a member, "uncommonly quick-sighted in seeing the weakness and defects of public men and measures." Yet he could be awed, for a moment at least. "I am among a consistory of kings," he wrote on July 4, 1776, a few days after arriving in Congress. "I assure you, sir, our Congress is an august assembly, and can they support the Declaration now on the anvil, they will be the greatest assembly on earth." He recovered quickly from that effusion. Mr. Clark composed "his countenance to more than usual gravity, to give more poignancy to his accustomed sarcasm," one man remarked upon his manner in debate.

Some felt Clark studied "more to please the people than to promote their real and permanent interests," an elaborate way of saying his colleagues found him to be a hair shirt. When Congress voted that all officers who had served in the Revolution should receive half pay for life, he called it an "injudicious act," "a measure contrary to the genius and political ideas of the New England states and New Jersey." He fought the decision the rest of the war against formidable opposition, and since it was never implemented he could claim the victory his. When Washington announced from military headquarters that all citizens of New Jersey who swore "allegiance to the United States" would be forgiven their political sins, Clark raised a storm in Congress. He objected that Tories could escape punishment by mouthing an oath. The people of New Jersey will "not tamely submit their authority to the control of a power unknown in our constitution," he went on. "We set out to oppose tyranny in all its strides, and I hope we shall persevere." Congress backed Washington, calling the oath a military necessity, but the General never again issued a similar edict.

Congress tolerated its hair shirt because he was "warmly attached to the liberties and independence of his country"—he could flail Washington's usurpation of a civilian power and at the same time exhaust himself working to channel supplies to the army—and also because he attended "to business and excelled in drawing up reports and resolutions." He had made a career of politics, and experience, coupled with tenacity and intelligence, made him hard to best in debate or on a committee.

Clark came from plain stock and never let the voters forget his origins. He did not so much seek to please the plain people, as accused, as to reflect and protect their interests. He was the son of a farmer and reared to be a farmer, but a "constitution naturally weak and a slender form prevented him from engaging in laborious pursuits." He became a surveyor. Sometimes landowners called in his rod and transit when a boundary dispute flared up, but usually it took a costly trip to court to settle matters. Clark detested pettifogging lawyers—a prejudice that provided abundant fuel for his sarcasm in Congress, a nest of lawyers—and after studying on his own began to dispense free legal advice. People called him the "Poor Man's Counsellor." Later, he pushed through the New Jersey legislature a law designed to shorten, and thereby reduce the cost of, legal procedures. The public called it "Clark's Law." "If it succeeds," he said, "it will tear off the ruffles from the lawyer's wrists."

When twenty-three years old he married an intrepid, enterprising girl who ran the family farm and reared their ten children while he gave all his time to politics. He eased into public life as county sheriff and was repeatedly re-elected to the post. While serving as a political fixture on the county level, he soaked up experience in the provincial scene as clerk of the assembly. He came out early for independence, and on June 22, 1776, New Jersey sent him to Congress to vote that opinion. A pair of formidable eyebrows called attention to his face, but otherwise the delegates found him unimpressive physically. Though never prosperous, he owned three slaves, and that gave him something in common with most men in Congress. Only the gregariousness natural to a politician made his righteous Presbyterianism and suspicious nature barely tolerable. His family thought him "very temperate," but he liked to drink. When Congress moved for a time to Baltimore, it stunned him to find "the poorest board, without any liquor, a dollar a day," and that the price of wine had soared to twelve shillings a bottle and rum to thirty shillings a gallon.

"As to my title, I know not yet whether it will be honorable or dishonorable," Clark wrote a friend a few days after signing the Declaration. "The issue of the war must settle it. Perhaps our Congress will be exalted on a high gallows." One thing, though, he knew for sure. "If we continued in the state we were in, it was evident we must perish; if we declared independence we might be saved." He ended the note with a characteristic postscript: "You'll please to accept this on plain paper; our dignity don't afford gilt, and our pay scarcely any."

John Hart
AGE: ABOUT 65   FARMER

The judgment of a colleague in Congress—"a plain, honest, well meaning Jersey farmer, with but little education, but with good sense and virtue eno' to discover and pursue the true interests of his country"—would have satisfied John Hart. Nor would he have quarreled with the succinct biography by a contemporary: "He was in personal appearance highly prepossessing, and in his younger days had been called handsome. His height was about five feet ten inches—his hair very black, his eyes light, and his complexion dark. The even tenor of his life was interrupted by few incidents that would not appear trivial in narration. His farm grew yearly better in value and improvement, his stock increased, his family was augmented by a biennial addition of a son or a daughter, until he was surrounded by thirteen children." He might have liked it known that along with the farm he owned grist and fulling mills. Also that he was a Baptist, the only one in Congress, but as "a sincere but unostentatious Christian" he would not have flaunted his uniqueness. Nor would he have insisted on being honored for signing the Declaration, although he paid heavily for the decision. When the British invaded New Jersey they ravaged his farm and mills, and as a most-wanted public enemy he was forced into hiding; for months he did not dare to see his family or to sleep two nights in a row in the same house.

Hart was born in Stonington, Connecticut but when still an infant his parents moved to Hopewell, New Jersey. His father was a farmer and he became one, too. He had done well enough by his mid-forties to become the leading citizen of his county. Local eminence and a reputation for abundant "good sense" carried him into public life as a justice of the peace, then regularly to the provincial assembly. He opposed all British efforts to tax the colonies, and by 1775 all the time he could spare from his farm went to politics; he served as a member of the provincial congress, the committee of correspondence, the committee of safety, and, although he lacked even a smattering of legal training, as a judge in the court of common pleas. In June 1776 the provincial congress elected him its vice president and then chose him to sit in the Second Congress. He made no impression there, for the month he signed the Declaration also saw him voted in as speaker of the New Jersey legislature re-created by the recently promulgated state constitution. He returned to the milieu of local politics, where he felt more comfortable and useful, and never again appeared in Congress.

Francis Hopkinson
AGE: 38   LAWYER

"I have a curiosity to penetrate a little deeper into the bosom of this curious gentleman," a delegate said after first meeting Hopkinson. "He is one of your pretty little, curious, ingenious men.

His head is not bigger than a large apple. . . . I have not met with anything in natural history much more amusing and entertaining than his personal appearance."

The times were strange indeed that could bring to Congress a man who, when forlorn with love, could write such ingeniously light lines as:

> My generous heart disdains
>   The slave of love to be;
> I scorn his servile chains,
>   And boast my liberty.
> This whining
> And pining
> And wasting with care,
> Are not to my taste, be she ever so fair.

To call him a lawyer only told how he earned a living. He played the harpsichord and had written original music for it. He dabbled with experiments in chemistry and physics. His light-hearted essays led some to say that posterity would find his power for satire "not unsurpassed by Lucian, Swift, or Rabelais." One friend thought the history of America's separation from Britain would "not be fully traced unless much is ascribed to the irresistible influence of the ridicule which he occasionally poured forth upon the enemies of those great political events."

Hopkinson was born in comfortable circumstances, the son of an immigrant from England who had become a successful Philadelphia lawyer, a friend of Franklin, and prominent in public affairs. But the father died when the boy was thirteen, and, although friends like Franklin helped where they could, Hopkinson was reared in genteel poverty. He attended the College of Philadelphia, which his father had helped found. After graduation he gave public concerts on the harpsichord, published poetry in the *American Magazine,* and studied law in the office of one of his father's friends. He was admitted to the bar when twenty-three, but showed little interest in building a practice. He shunned politics but made it clear he welcomed political preferment, and through family connections in England won his first sinecure—collector of customs at Salem, New Jersey. It was a modest post, and after repeal of the Stamp Act Hopkinson sailed for England to seek something better. Lord North told him he had nothing to offer until the stamp agents deprived of their jobs were taken care of. Five years passed before Hopkinson became collector of customs at New Castle, Delaware. Meanwhile, he had married Ann Borden of New Jersey, whose well-to-do family had founded Bordentown. He settled there and with help from her family prospered as a lawyer. Governor William Franklin appointed him to the prestigious provincial council.

All the while he accepted royal favors with one hand, with the other he turned out a stream of gentle satires against British oppression that he published under a variety of pseudonyms. In the spring of 1776 he produced "The Prophecy," an allegory that revolved around "a certain tree," royal government, planted many years earlier by the king in America. It was prophesied the people would cultivate the tree with care and "worship it as a god." But then "there shall arise a North wind, and shall blast the tree, so that it shall no longer yield its fruit, or afford shelter to the people, but it shall become rotten at the heart." Eventually "the people shall root up the rotten tree, and in its place they shall plant a young and vigorous tree, and shall effectually defend it from the winds of the North by an high wall. And they shall dress it, and prune it, and cultivate it to their own liking. And the young tree shall grow and flourish and spread its branches far abroad; and the people shall dwell under the shadow of its branches, and shall become an exceeding great, and powerful, and happy nation. And of their increase there shall be no end."

Hopkinson came to Congress only in time to vote for independence and thereafter contributed little that was substantial. Yet no one spoke ill of him. The delegates welcomed his sociable presence. "He possessed uncommon talents for pleasing in company," said a member. "His wit was not of that coarse kind which sets 'a table in a roar,' but it was mild, delicate, and elegant, and infusing cheerfulness rather than mirth in all who heard it. . . . He was so agreeable and kind as a neighbor that he constantly created friends in every part of the city in which he resided. His domestic character was unsullied by any of the imperfections which sometimes cleave to genius." Such was the charm of Hopkinson that even a rigid Presbyterian in Congress could pass lightly over the rumor that the genteel little man "was suspected of inclining to deism."

None in Congress expected another great debate on July 1. All assumed "that argument had been exhausted on both sides." But John Dickinson insisted on a last plea against declaring independence at this time. "It is our interest to keep Great Britain in the opinion that we mean reconciliation as long as possible," he told his colleagues. The fragile-looking Dickinson, "slender as a reed, pale as ashes," was an eloquent speaker, and those wavering on the question listened attentively. He asked what was to be gained from a declaration of independence. Some say it might "animate the people" and arouse the troops; that it would convince "foreign powers of our strength and unanimity" and persuade them to send "aid in consequence thereof"; that it would cement the colonies into a firm union. It would do none of these things, said Dickinson. "The preservation of life, liberty, and property is sufficient motive to animate the people." Foreign powers will not rely on words; they want deeds. A declaration of independence will splinter, not strengthen, the union. He predicted that a "partition of these colonies will take place" and the United States would not long survive as a free nation. "I should be glad to know whether in twenty or thirty years this commonwealth of colonies may not be thought too unwieldy, and Hudson's River be a proper boundary for a separate commonwealth to the northward. I have a strong impression this will take place." It especially saddened him, he said, pointing at the paper Jefferson had written, which lay on a desk nearby, to see Congress confronted with a Declaration "so vehemently written." We must not "brave the storm" that lies ahead in "this skiff made of paper."

When Dickinson sat down, John Hancock prepared to call for a vote on the question. Instead, Richard Stockton rose and said his colleagues from New Jersey "had been attentive to what had been passing abroad, but they had not heard the arguments in Congress and did not incline to give their opinions until they should hear the sentiments of members there." Edward Rutledge stepped over to John Adams. "Nobody will speak but you on this subject," he said, smiling. "You have all the topics so ready, that you must satisfy the gentlemen from New Jersey."

Adams smiled in return, and he said later that "it had so much the air of exhibiting like an actor or gladiator, for the entertainment of the audience, that I was shamed to repeat what I had said twenty times before, and I thought nothing new could be advanced by me." But urged on by the whole room, he spoke. He said nothing new but clothed old arguments with such eloquence that those who listened called it the greatest speech ever heard in Congress. "The man to whom the country is most indebted for the great measure of independence," Richard Stockton said later, "is Mr. John Adams of Boston—I call him the Atlas of Independence.— He it was who sustained the debate, and by the force of his reasonings, demonstrated not only the justice but the expediency of the measure."

Adams left little for anyone else to say. During the afternoon the question of independence was put to an informal vote. The result showed nine colonies for independence, two against—Pennsylvania and South Carolina—and one, Delaware, with its delegation down to two men, evenly split. New York had abstained from voting. The delegation announced it favored independence but their instructions from their home legislature forbade them to promote any measure that blocked the chance for reconciliation. "They therefore thought themselves not justified in voting on either side, and asked leave to withdraw from the question, which was given them."

No one in Congress—not even John Dickinson—had resisted independence harder than Edward Rutledge. But he had seen the tide turn against him during the three-week grace period wangled from colleagues, and now, unlike Dickinson, he decided to swing with it gracefully. After the unofficial vote had been tallied, he asked that a formal vote be postponed until the next day. He wanted time to persuade the recalcitrant members of his delegation to change their votes. His request was quickly granted. Others hoped that Caesar Rodney, still absent, might be brought up from Delaware in time to break the deadlock in his delegation. And if sufficient pressure were applied to Pennsylvania, possibly by morning the hesitant members of that delegation might have changed their position. John Adams hoped for unanimity the next day, "yet I cannot promise this," he said. "Because one or two gentlemen may possibly be found who will vote point blank against the known and declared sense of the constituents."

10

The Roll Call

Tuesday morning, July 2, the delegates walked through a heavy rain to the State House. Most of them had arrived and unwrapped themselves from their rain garments and entered the meeting room when Caesar Rodney, still in his boots and spurs, clattered up to the door. In response to a note from McKean that his vote was needed to break the deadlock in the Delaware delegation he had ridden eighty miles through a rain-swept night.

Caesar Rodney
AGE: 48   POLITICIAN

He seemed a solemn gentleman, blood brother to Roger Sherman and Samuel Adams, when judged by his letters, wherein he talked much about the "manly opposition" of Americans "to those vile invaders of their just rights, privileges and property," those "enemies to our righteous cause," "those sappers of the rights of mankind." Colleagues in Congress saw a different man, a good-humored, carefree bachelor, fond of company and filled with gaiety. He liked to drink, or, as a contemporary phrased it, was "not averse to the pleasures of the table, never exceeding, however, the boundaries of propriety and good manners." One delegate found him "the oddest looking man in the world," a long, pale reed with a head perched on top "not bigger than a large apple." When describing him colleagues courteously overlooked the cancerous sore that had begun to spread down one side of Rodney's face. They saw instead the "sense and fire, spirit, wit, and humor in his countenance."

That humor could puncture even the formidable Harrison, whose tedious eulogies upon the glories of his dominion of Virginia had led irked Northern delegates to coin the word "dominionism" as a synonym for fulsome praise. One day when it looked as though the war might shift to the South, Harrison painted a picture of his province for Congress in colors less bright than usual. He demanded arms and men, and in massive quantities. Virginia, it now appeared was "destitute in every point and circumstance." "When he sat down there was a momentary silence, all being surprised that such a development should come from Harrison," a colleague recalled. Rodney rose to reply. He was at the time little more than an animated scarecrow, "decorated with a bandage, from which was suspended the green silk covering over one eye, to hide the ravages of his cancer," but the crocodile tears brimming in his eyes stifled any thought of pity. The melancholy state of the once powerful dominion of Virginia was truly deplorable, he told Harrison. "But," he went on—and here his voice rose "an octave higher than concert pitch"—"but, let her be of good cheer; she has a friend in need; DELAWARE will take her under its protection, and insure her safety." Congress exploded with laughter and Harrison, deflated but relishing the joke, joined in.

That humor, coupled with intelligence and energy, had carried Rodney through twenty years of Delaware politics, a career that began when he became high sheriff of Kent County at the age of twenty-seven. Whatever political posts the county had to offer —register of wills, recorder of deeds, clerk of the orphans' court, justice of the peace—Rodney received. When he was thirty-three the county began electing him regularly to the provincial assembly. The assembly showed its respect by sending him with Thomas McKean to the Stamp Act Congress, which met in New York in 1765. (Later when the two reminisced about the gathering, McKean sputtered about the dishonorable behavior of Timothy Ruggles of Massachusetts while Rodney, characteristically, only "made merry with Ruggles" in his anecdotes.) At the age of forty-one he was chosen speaker by the assembly, and the governor appointed him to the supreme court, though he lacked legal training.

Rodney attended the First Congress. When he returned to the Second, he found all his old friends—John Dickinson, Robert Morris, George Read—opposed to independence, but for Rodney "it was difficult to say what might be best." He saw on the one side "a bloody war and on the other unconditional submission to the power of Great Britain," both dreadful options. He listened to the debates on independence through the spring of 1776 without committing himself. Finally, he was convinced that Britain "was making every kind of exertion in her power to reduce us to unconditional submission; all her conduct so fully induced this intention that no hope of reconciliation on constitutional principles could possibly remain."

In late June 1776 Rodney was in Delaware—as speaker of the provincial convention he served in effect as the colony's chief executive officer and often had to hasten home to put out political brush fires—when he received letters from Read and McKean urging him to hurry back to Congress, where "important business" was about to be decided.

Thomas McKean met him as he entered the State House, and "after a friendly salutation (without a word on the business) we went into the hall of Congress together, and found we were among the latest; proceedings immediately commenced, and after a few minutes the great question was put."

Secretary Thomson began the roll call as usual with New Hampshire, reading off the colonies from North to South. Josiah Bartlett cast the first vote. Tradition has it "he boldly answered in the affirmative." No one recorded the individual votes, but it is certain no one heard a "nay" as Thomson went through each New England delegation. New York, still uninstructed from home, once more abstained.

Pennsylvania: two "nays" and three "ayes," which put the colony's vote in the "aye" column. To prevent a deadlock in the delegation, John Dickinson had stayed away that morning. So, too, had Robert Morris.

$\mathscr{R}$obert $\mathscr{M}$orris
AGE: 42   MERCHANT

"You ask me what you are to think of Robert Morris?" a delegate wrote when Morris was doing his best to delay a decision for independence. "I will tell you what I think of him. I think he has a masterly understanding, an open temper and an honest heart; and if he does not always vote for what you and I should think proper, it is because he thinks that a large body of people remains, who are not yet of his mind. He has vast designs in the mercantile way. And no doubt pursues mercantile ends, which are always gain; but he is an excellent member of our body."

Those "vast designs in the mercantile way" would one day undo Morris. Not many months passed before a fellow member accused him of being among those who make "patriotism the stalking horse to their private interests." But in 1776 colleagues had only praise for him—"his perceptions were quick and his judgment sound upon all subjects," one recalled—and handed him enough work to keep ten men busy. "I have been amazed how you waded thro' it and found leisure for your own private concerns and the enjoyment of your friends," a friend wrote. "Congress seems unanimously sensible of the obligations which they owe you, and you may boast of being the only man whom they all agree to speak and I really believe think well of."

Morris cared little for popularity unless it could be converted into money, power, or prestige. These he courted from youth. A politician once asked about his childhood, answered, "it was the usual sort—disastrous." Morris might have made the remark. He was born in Liverpool, England, and lived close to poverty until he was thirteen, when he joined his father in Maryland. His father, happily settled with a mistress, sent him to school in Philadelphia. After acquiring only a veneer of education the boy went to work for a family of shipping merchants, the Willings. He was a tall, strong young man with a quick mind, bottomless energy, and an aggressive drive cloaked with a quiet manner which, "though not highly polished," was "free from the least tincture of vulgarity." He suffered from a "terrifying malady," asthma, but fought it as hard as he fought for material success. ("Exercise at the pump was the specific which he resorted to, and he often labored as though he were assisting to save a sinking vessel. He, however, by this means, frequently obtained relief from violent paroxysms, in a few moments.") When Morris was twenty years old, the Willing family changed the name of the firm to Willing, Morris and Company.

During the next decade Morris built the company into one of the most prestigious and profitable in the colonies. He stayed clear of politics, except for an unobtrusive role in the opposition against the Stamp Act, and also of marriage until the age of thirty-five. He was "most affectionately attached" to his wife. The house he built for her "is handsome, closely resembling the houses in London," a visitor remarked; "he lives there without ostentation, but not without expense, for he spares nothing which can contribute to his happiness, and that of Mrs. Morris. . . ."

In the ten years following the Stamp Act Morris concentrated on business, with only a sidelong glance at politics until the battle at Lexington. Two and a half months later he accepted an ap-

The Roll Call 159

pointment to the provincial council of safety, then stood for and won a seat in the assembly. The assembly sent him to the Second Congress. "Ambition had no share in bringing me forward into public life, nor has it any charms to keep me there," he said. Within two or three months he had been assigned to every congressional committee that could use his commercial experience. For a newcomer to public life he appeared a surprisingly "bold, sensible, and agreeable speaker" on the floor of Congress. He argued relentlessly for reconciliation. "If I have any influence or should hereafter gain any, it shall be exerted in favor of every measure that has a tendency to procure accommodation on terms consistent with our just claims," he said. He still held out for reconciliation on July 1 and voted against independence when Congress, sitting as a committee of the whole, was polled. He absented himself from the chamber when the formal vote came the next day. "My opposition was founded in the evil consequences I foresaw, or thought I foresaw," he said. He also objected to the timing of the decision, fearing independence would lead to disputes "about liberties, privileges, posts, and places at the very time we ought to have nothing in view but the securing of those objects and placing them on such a footing as to make them worth contending for amongst themselves hereafter."

Still, on August 2 Morris signed the Declaration. "I am not one of those testy politicians that run resty when my own plans are not adopted," he explained, "for I think it the duty of a good citizen to follow when he cannot lead." A year later he confessed from the floor in Congress "that he had been mistaken in his former opinion as to its time, and said that it would have been better for our country had it been declared sooner."

"Delaware"—Rodney rose and gave a short speech that ended with the words "I vote for independence." McKean voted "aye." George Read voted "nay."

George Read

AGE: 42   LAWYER

He believed that an early marriage impeded the progress of an ambitious man, and he did not wed until after his twenty-ninth birthday, when success as a lawyer was assured. The same cautious deliberation shaped Read's vote on independence. He thought the incalculable dangers presented by a "leap in the dark" could, for a time at least, be postponed until one more attempt at reconciliation had been made. His stand did little to injure his reputation in Congress. "A shrewd lawyer, of gentle manner, and of considerable talents and knowledge," said a colleague who voted on the opposite side of the question. "He was firm, without violence, in all his purposes, and was much respected by all his acquaintances."

Read was reared in New Castle, Delaware, by Presbyterian parents who saw that he got an orthodox education from a sound clergyman. They sent him when fifteen to read law in Philadelphia. He was admitted to the bar when twenty and began to practice in Philadelphia. Like James Wilson and his brother-in-law to be, George Ross, he saw that advancement in a city crowded with competent lawyers would be unbearably slow. He returned to New Castle and during the next nine years built one of the most lucrative practices in the Lower Counties, as Delaware was then called. In court "he was somewhat slow in speech, and negligent in manner, but his profound legal knowledge, his clear reasoning, gave him an influence with juries and judges."

Read took few risks. He chose for a wife a girl he had known for many years who had recently become a widow. They were unusually compatible. He wrote regularly while away from home, assuring her that "if anything very material occurs you shall hear of it." The affectionate relations with his wife and the five children she eventually gave him did not extend much beyond the family boundary. "He avoided trifling occupation, disliked familiarity," it was said, "and could not tolerate the slightest violation of good manners, for which he was himself distinguished."

Three months after his marriage he became attorney general for Delaware and a short while later a member of the provincial assembly. He held both posts until the Revolution. As attorney general he opposed the Stamp Act and predicted that if Parliament persisted in the effort to make "slaves" out of the colonists they would eventually seek "to live as independent of Great Britain as possible." Read never blustered, but from then on he quietly opposed British imperial policy. The legislature without hesitation chose him for the First and then the Second Congress.

The congressional work load astonished him. "The day is consumed this way," he wrote his wife, ". . . shaving, washing, breakfasting," then "hurrying to Congress, sitting there till three o'clock," pausing for dinner, attending committee meetings in the evening, the day's work ending sometime around nine o'clock with the sedate Read "walking quickly home to avoid the night air." Despite attention to duty, Read believed he had a reputation for negligence. "I was yesterday put upon a committee that is to meet every evening at six o'clock," he told his wife, "which may be obliged to sit regularly for ten days to come, and as I am considered a great absentee heretofore, I must attend constantly for a while."

By early January 1776 he confessed to being "almost worn down" by the "multiplicity of business." He had hardly returned home for a rest when William Hooper wrote pleading for him to hasten back to Congress. The vote of every moderate man was needed to block the growing strength of those for independence. Read returned at once and except for a holiday in March attended regularly down to the day Congress voted on independence. Up to that moment he and Rodney had seen eye to eye on all major issues. Now they parted. Read voted "nay" when his turn came. His decision was not generally known outside Congress until twenty years later when Thomas McKean revealed that "for Delaware my vote was for independence; my colleague George Read, Esquire, voted against it." Within Congress at the time, however, "some of the most sagacious men," according to one who later became a political enemy, "pronounced him better fitted for the district of *St. James's* than the region of *America.*"

Read on July 2 felt that postponing independence kept alive the possibility of "reconciliation on constitutional principles." Also, like other men of property, he was more "alarmed with the horrors of civil war" than the glory of an equal and separate station for America among the nations of the world. Why, then, a month later did he sign the Declaration? "To avoid singularity," goes one explanation. More to the point, not to have signed would have been political suicide. Accepting the Declaration was, in effect, taking an oath of loyalty to the new nation. Refusing to sign it would have forced Read to leave Congress and politics and thereby abandon the chance to direct his state and the nation down the path he wished them to take. The public's ignorance of his vote on independence allowed him, soon after signing, to win a seat in Delaware's constitutional convention, where as presiding officer and a member of the drafting committee he directed the creation of a new government essentially like the one Delaware had always lived under. That pleased Read.

"Virginia"—Richard Henry Lee and George Wythe were absent; they were back in Virginia helping to construct a constitution. Harrison, "aye." Jefferson, "aye." Francis Lightfoot Lee, "aye." Thomas Nelson, "aye." Carter Braxton—if there was a negative vote in the delegation, it was his.

Carter Braxton
AGE: 39   COUNTRY GENTLEMAN

"He was a decent, agreeable, and sensible speaker, and in private life an accomplished gentleman," a colleague said. "He was not deficient in political information, but was suspected of being less detached than he should be from his British prejudices." True, Braxton did have a prejudice for things British. After his first wife died in childbirth, he spent three years in England refining his tastes. He returned home to marry the British-born daughter of the king's receiver-general of customs in Virginia. (Later, as the colonies edged toward independence, "the extreme, imprudent and inimical conduct of his lady" aroused unfavorable comment even from Jefferson, who rarely retailed gossip.) He accommodated his family of two children from the first marriage and what eventually amounted to sixteen from the second, ten of whom lived to maturity, in two elegant mansions which his great wealth in land and slaves allowed him to furnish with the best that could be imported from Britain.

Upon his return to America Braxton did what society expected of him—entered the House of Burgesses. He served there until the governor dissolved it in 1774, then transferred his allegiance to the extralegal provincial convention. He served on the colony's committee of safety until the convention early in 1776 sent him to the Second Congress. He arrived there believing the imperial machinery might here and there need repairing but that it would be madness to discard it completely. Separation from Britain he saw as "a delusive bait which men inconsiderately catch at, without knowing the hook to which it is affixed." His "British prejudices" helped him to resist the bait. Also his hatred of New Englanders. ("I hate their government—I hate their religion—I hate their levelling.") But there were other reasons that outweighed personal prejudices, and in passing them along in a letter to a relative Braxton spoke cogently for all those in Congress who opposed independence on practical grounds:

It is an object to be wished for by every American, when it can be obtained with safety and honor. . . . That ᐧthis is not the moment I will prove by arguments that to me are decisive, and which exist with certainty. Your refined notion of our public honor being engaged to await the terms offered by [peace] commissioners operates strongly with me and many others and makes the first reason I would offer.

My next is that America is in too defenseless a state for the declaration, having no alliance with a naval power nor as yet any fleet of consequence of her own to protect that trade which is so essential to the prosecution of the war, without which I know we cannot go on much longer. It is said by advocates for separation that France will undoubtedly assist us after we have asserted the state, and therefore they urge us to make the experiment. Would such a blind, precipitate measure as this be justified by prudence? —first to throw off our connection with Great Britain and then give ourselves up to the arms of France. Would not the court so famous for intrigues and deception avail herself of our situation and from it exact much severer terms than if we were to treat with her (Great Britain) before hand and settle the terms of any future alliance? Surely she would, but the truth of the matter is, there are some who are afraid to await the arrival of commissioners, lest the dispute should be accommodated much against their will even upon the admission of our own terms.

For however strange it may appear, I am satisfied that the eastern colonies [New England] do not mean to have a reconciliation and in this I am justified by public and private reasons. Two of the New England colonies [Rhode Island and Connecticut] enjoy a government purely democratical, the nature and principle of which, both civil and religious, are so totally incompatible with monarchy, that they have ever lived in a restless state under it. The other two, tho' not so popular in their frame, bordered so near upon it that monarchical influence hung very heavy on them. The best opportunity in the world being now offered them to throw off all subjection and embrace their darling democracy, they are determined to accept it.

A danger worse than democracy—civil war—threatened to materialize with independence, Braxton warned. Connecticut has "at this time eight hundred men in arms" to defend its claim to land inside Pennsylvania's borders. Meanwhile, other land disputes simmer away: between Virginia and Pennsylvania, Maryland and Virginia, New York and New Hampshire over the land of the Green Mountains. "And yet without any adjustment of those disputes and a variety of other matters," Braxton continues, "some are for lugging us into independence. But so long as these remain unsettled and men act upon the principles they ever have done, you may rely no such thing will be generally agreed on.

"Upon reviewing the secret movements of men and things I am convinced the assertion of independence is far off. If it was to be now asserted, the continent would be torn in pieces by intestine wars and convulsions. Previous to independence all disputes must be healed and harmony prevail. A grand continental league must be formed and a superintending power also. When these necessary steps are taken and I see a coalition formed sufficient to withstand the power of Britain, or any other, then am I for an independent state and all its consequences, as then I think they will produce happiness to America. It is a true saying of a wit—'we must hang together or separately.' "

Seventy-nine days after Braxton predicted that "the assertion of independence is far off," Congress declared the colonies to be free states. There is no record of how Braxton voted, but a month later he signed the embossed copy of the Declaration, then left for home, never again to return to Congress.

"North Carolina"—Penn, "aye." Hewes, "aye." The unanimous vote was possible only because William Hooper stayed away that morning.

William Hooper
AGE: 34   LAWYER

He seemed an anomoly to colleagues in Congress: a Southerner who spoke with a New England accent, an early patriot who refused to vote for independence when the day came, then four weeks later signed the Declaration. Thomas Jefferson and he were "intimate and familiar" friends, yet Jefferson blighted his reputation forever. "You remember as well as I do," he said late in life to John Adams, "that we had not a greater Tory in Congress than Hooper."

Hooper was born in Boston, the son of a clergyman determined to give his child as a tithe to the church. He entered Harvard when thirteen and learned "to despise the cant of divines, and the pride and hypocrisy of the schools." He shone as an orator and decided, despite importunities from his father, to become a lawyer. He read law in the office of the mercurial James Otis, an early spokesman for freedom and liberty. Convinced Boston had no room for another lawyer, he went to Wilmington, North Carolina, when he was twenty-two. His patron there, a family friend, thought he would do well "if he has prudence, which is doubted." Prudence came quickly in an unexpected way—he fell in love with a plain but uncommonly charming girl named Anne Clark, ever afterward his "dear Annie." Her family and his opposed their desire to wed. Both sides agreed that first Hooper must be domesticated politically. Strings were pulled, and he became North Carolina's attorney general. He conducted himself with "uncommon firmness and assiduity," and after a year in the post the couple were permitted to marry.

Hooper converted to Southern life with ease. He joined the Anglican Church. He acquired a modest plantation outside Wilmington with a dozen or so slaves. When homesick, he who had been reared in the land of cod yearned to "eat my hog and hominy." Parliament's closing of the Boston port after the dumping of the tea revived affection for his "native country," as he called Massachusetts. "Infatuated people!" he said of those who thought Boston could be starved into submission. "Do they imagine that we will make a tame surrender of all that an honest man ought to hold dear without a struggle to preserve; and that our pretensions to freedom are chimerical?" He helped raise £2000 and two shiploads of provisions for his beleaguered town.

The North Carolina legislature sent its adopted son to the First Congress, where one member judged him "polite, spirited, and tolerably eloquent" and another ranked him with Richard Henry Lee and Patrick Henry as an orator. Reactions to him as a person were mixed. Among those he was friendly with he "shone with luster whenever he pleased to exert himself" and he could be "hospitable to excess." Others noticed he "had much nervous irritability" and in conversation could be "frequently sarcastic and severe." And blunt, too. "The Council of Safety, a set of water gruel sons of b——s, told the people a damned lie," he remarked in one letter.

Although the accent was Boston's, he spoke for North Carolina. In an early debate he took time to explain that his colony's main products were tar, pitch, and turpentine, which could be marketed only in England and that "Britain cannot do without." The South's peculiar institution embarrassed him, and he hoped "to see the day that slaves are not necessary," but he had a Southerner's view of the black man. "White and Negroes cannot work together," he said. "Negroes are goods and chattels, are property. A Negro works under the impulse of fear—has no care of his master's interest."

Hooper looked younger than his age. A delegate three years his junior called him a "sprightly young lawyer." His features were "delicate and well formed," but there was strength beneath the fragile exterior and in the Second Congress colleagues handed him an outsized share of assignments. "You ask 'what is become of Hooper?'" he wrote home. "I answer he is the packhorse of North Carolina, carrying his burden in Congress all day, and varying it only by taking it up in committees all evening. In a word, I am fatigued almost to death. . . . I never in my life felt myself so perfectly exculpated from the sin of omission. I am at a loss to conceive how I have found time to write so many public and private letters."

Hooper turned on his "native country" as Congress edged toward independence. "I am wearied of bloodsuckers," he said when a delegate pressed for a special bounty for Massachusetts volunteers. "I care not how soon I am relieved from them." When New England privateers seized ships owned by citizens of North Carolina, he felt that "the defenseless Southern colonies [had] become a devoted prey to their more formidable Eastern neighbors." As those who favored reconciliation, as he did, lost ground, Hooper lost heart. "I am weary of politics," he wrote on January 6, 1776, three days before *Common Sense* was published. "It is a study that corrupts the human heart, degrades the idea of human nature, and drives men to expedients that morality must condemn; deep strategems, dark disguise, fiction, falsehood, are but the fair side of the picture of a perfect politician." He continued to denounce Loyalists as "infernal villains," but behind the invective lay a distraught man. His brother had declared himself a Loyalist, and from that moment the American Revolution became for Hooper a civil war. (Later when the brothers attempted a reconciliation Hooper confessed "our meeting was awkward, distant and distressing to me.") Only one man, "the greatest man on earth," gave him hope for the future—George Washington. "Misfortunes are the element in which he shines," he said. He alone had thus far rescued America "from ruin by the mere strength of his genius, conduct, and courage, encountering every obstacle that want of money, men, arms, ammunition, could throw in his way."

He feared that even Washington could not prevent a war for independence from turning into a real revolution, bringing in "an execrable democracy" that would "shake the very being of this once flourishing country." He feared, too, that independence would divide the nation much as the war had split apart his family. On July 2 Hooper could not bring himself to vote for separation, but like his friend Robert Morris he stayed away from Congress in order that North Carolina might fall into the "aye" column. Four weeks later he had resigned himself to the decision of Congress and, again like Robert Morris, put his name to the Declaration. "There will be a time and I hope it is not at a great distance," he told Morris, "when the distinction of Whig and Tory will be lost and resolve itself into the common appellation of *Citizens of the Independent States*. All political grudges will die away and harmony and happiness cement the whole. I wish that no wound may be made among ourselves that time and common interest may not at last heal."

"South Carolina"—If there was a negative vote in the delegation, it was most likely that of Thomas Lynch, Jr.

Thomas Lynch, Jr.
AGE: 27   COUNTRY GENTLEMAN

The son only served as his father's proxy. Thomas Lynch, Sr., had impressed Congress and would have signed the Declaration if his hand could have held the pen. John Adams had met the old man —though only forty-six at the time, he looked "about sixty"—in Boston and judged him "an hearty friend to America and her righteous cause." Adams continued "vastly pleased with Mr. Lynch" at the First Congress. "He is a solid, firm, judicious man." He has "an immense fortune," another New Englander reported, but "is plain, sensible, above ceremony, and carries with him more force in his very appearance than most powdered folks in their conversation. He wears his hair straight, his clothes in the plainest order, and is highly esteemed."

Judgments changed in the Second Congress. There Adams watched Lynch begin "to waver and clamor" about independence, and Lynch, in turn, wondered "whether [Adams'] intentions be wicked or not" and warned "he should be watched." Lynch headed the band of reconciliationists in Congress until felled by a paralytic stroke in February 1776. South Carolina promptly sent the son to Congress to be with and speak for his father. Young Lynch did not impress Congress. "A man of moderate talents and timid in difficult circumstances of his country," a delegate reported.

Thomas Lynch, Jr., had been reared as a spoiled, only child of a domineering but adoring father. He had been exposed to the tour of duty in England required of South Carolina's gentlemen. His lasted eight years. He began at Eton, moved on to Cambridge, and ended in London with a stretch at the Middle Temple reading law. When he returned home and told his father he did not want to become a lawyer, the wish was honored, but no further deviations from the mold that had been cast for Southern gentlemen would be allowed. After he had married a suitable belle and taken on the management of the plantation his father gave him, he must enter public life. His father managed his election to the provincial assembly. But young Lynch did not sparkle in the role custom called on him to act out. "Among his faults," said an admiring but defensive contemporary, "it might be said that he was too much addicted to the indulgence of that literary lounging, which, when urged to an extreme, found it difficult to excite him to exertion in public, more especially as this habit, cooperating with his great modesty, frequently produced an almost invincible reluctance to display himself." The boy disappointed his father in other ways. His marriage produced no children. Equally sad, his modesty proved too great. An appointment as captain in a provincial regiment pleased him but not his father, who thought the rank demeaning and wanted to pull strings that would win a quick promotion; the son refused to allow it. Sadder still, the young man while on a recruiting trip in North Carolina came down with a puzzling fever he could not shake and which left him a semi-invalid.

In Congress, however, Thomas, Jr., pleased his father. There he spoke as a true son of South Carolina. "Our slaves [are] our property," he said in one of his rare speeches. "Freemen cannot be got to work in our colonies. It is not in the ability or inclination of freemen to do the work that the Negroes do." He was present in Congress on July 2, but it is not known how he voted on independence. If his bed-ridden father still preached against separation, then the son opposed independence. That he was judged "timid in difficult circumstances" suggests he voted "nay." If so, he had become reconciled to the decision of Congress by August 2 when, as much for his father as for himself, he signed the Declaration.

"Georgia"—"Aye."

Without a single colony dissenting and only one abstaining the United Colonies had voted themselves independent. Charles Thomson now wrote in the official journal of Congress:

Resolved, That these United Colonies are, and, of right, ought to be Free and Independent States; that they are absolved from all allegiance to the British crown, and that all political connexion between them and the state of Great Britain is, and ought to be, totally dissolved.

"The Second of July 1776 will be the most memorable epocha in the history of America," John Adams said soon after the vote. "I am apt to believe that it will be celebrated by succeeding generations as the great anniversary festival. It ought to be commemorated, as the day of deliverance, by solemn acts of devotion to God Almighty. It ought to be solemnized with pomp and parade, with shows, games, sports, guns, bells, bonfires, and illuminations, from one end of this continent to the other, from this time forward forevermore."

He went on, "You will think me transported with enthusiasm, but I am not. I am well aware of the toil and blood and treasure that it will cost us to maintain this Declaration and support and defend these states. Yet, through all the gloom, I can see the rays of ravishing light and glory. I can see that the end is more than worth all the means. And that posterity will triumph in that day's transactions, even although we should rue it, which I trust in God we shall not."

Caesar Rodney had been in politics too long to allow himself to be carried away by the event. "I arrived in Congress (tho' detained by thunder and rain) time enough to give my voice in the matter of independence," he said in a brief note to his brother. "It is determined by the thirteen

United Colonies, without even one dissenting colony." A final sentence dealt with another important matter. "Don't neglect to attend closely and carefully to my harvest and you'll oblige."

11
∾

A Difficult Time for
Mr. Jefferson

Congress began to edit Jefferson's Declaration of Independence in the early afternoon of July 2 and continued to revise, amend, and cut the paper through the next two days. No author likes to have someone he thinks knows little about writing slash away at his sentences; he likes it less if the surgery is performed in public. Jefferson recorded that Benjamin Franklin, "who perceived that I was not insensible to these mutilations," leaned over from his adjacent seat and tried to divert him with a story.

Benjamin Franklin
AGE: 70   RETIRED PRINTER

The news of Lexington was still the talk of the town when Benjamin Franklin returned from England on May 5, 1775. His arrival in Philadelphia was "announced by ringing of bells, to the great joy of the city," and the provincial assembly, then in session, instantly added his name to the Pennsylvania delegation chosen for the Second Congress. When Congress convened four days later, Franklin was in his seat. For over two decades delegates had heard about the "prodigious genius" of Doctor Franklin. His "iron points" dotted roof tops in every village. He had lived in England some sixteen years and come home a man of world renown, the single American whose name was familiar in every household the length of the land. Now here he sat, "a short, fat trunched old man in a plain dress, bald pate, and short white locks." And he sat saying nothing, in *"expressive silence."*

So great was his reputation that men hardly dared to consider what the effect would have been if, within a few days after his return, Franklin had announced for or against independence. But such an "if" would have required him to act against his nature. He had never been a man to hurry a decision and now, nearly seventy, he was even less prone to haste. Nor was he eager to find himself on the losing side of a cause. "Didst thee ever know Dr. Franklin to be in a minority?" a Quaker once asked rhetorically. So Franklin held his peace until he saw what was best for his interests and America's.

The first month and a half he kept to his house and went abroad only on public business. Those for reconciliation hoped he would use his influence to make Congress act with moderation. Rumors circulated that he planned soon to sail back to London on a peace mission, then his long silence evoked gossip of another sort. It was whispered about the city that the delegates in Congress "begin to entertain a great suspicion that Dr. Franklin came rather as a spy than as a friend, and that he means to discover our weak side to make his peace with the ministers by discovering information with regard to affairs at home, but hitherto he has been silent on that head and in every respect behaved more like a spectator than a member." A British agent in Philadelphia knew Franklin was no spy, but he knew little else. "By every intelligence I can get," he reported home in May, "Dr. Franklin keeps much on the reserve, and has not hitherto opined in the manner that was expected; if he is not blinded by faction, he can be of more use to Great Britain and America than any man in this country." A month later the spy reported that Franklin remained "among those who are for moderation, and bringing about reconciliatory measures, but," he added "as he is a deep, designing man, it is not easy coming at his real intentions." Franklin's reticence "highly offended" the volatile Richard Henry Lee of Virginia.

The rumors had died away by mid-July. By then he had told his old political ally Joseph Galloway and his son William, governor of New Jersey—both of whom would become Loyalists—that he favored independence. "The suspicions against Dr. Franklin have died away," a citizen reported; "whatever his design at coming over here, I believe he has now chosen his side, and favors our cause." But he did little inside and nothing outside Congress to promote independence, made no public speeches, wrote no articles for the press. The people must decide the question without his help.

"Dr. Franklin has been very constant in his attendance on Congress from the beginning," John Adams told his wife on July 23, and then proceeded to chart the doctor's curious course with a precision and clarity even Franklin would have admired.

His conduct has been composed and grave and in the opinion of many gentlemen very reserved. He has not assumed anything, nor affected to take the lead; but has seemed to choose that the Congress should pursue their own principles and sentiments and adopt their own plans. Yet he has not been backward; has been very useful on many occasions, and discovered a disposition entirely American. He does not hesitate at our boldest measures, but rather seems to think us too irresolute and backward. He thinks us at present in an odd state, neither in peace nor war, neither dependent nor independent. But he thinks that we shall soon assume a character more decisive.

He thinks that we have the power of preserving ourselves, and that even if we should be driven to the disagreeable necessity of assuming a total independency, and set up a separate state, we could maintain it. The people of England have thought that the opposition in America was wholly owing to Dr. Franklin; and I suppose their scribblers will attribute the temper and proceedings of this Congress to him; but there cannot be a greater mistake. He has had but little share farther than to cooperate and assist.

Although Franklin, like Adams, had been reared in Massachusetts, he resembled no man ever met there by Adams, who never came close to understanding him. "More of a philosopher than a politician," he said of one of the most adept politicians in Congress, Samuel Adams not excepted. A politician to Adams, who thought politics to be a noble profession, took a firm stand on an issue, then fought for it. Franklin, however, when he saw others headed in the direction he was going, husbanded his energy, satisfied "to cooperate and assist" while his companions fought the battles. Adams raged at Franklin's "passion for reputation and fame," which even friends admitted to be one of the old man's weaknesses, but failed to see that he used that fame deftly for ends beyond the reach of lesser mortals. James Wilson had a story to prove it. There was a citizen who once proposed to divert the waters of a creek north of Philadelphia into the city for public use. The man was carried by his family into court "to prove him insane." Later Franklin donated £1000 to get the project underway, "and obtained for his legacy the character of a wise and benevolent man."

On committees Franklin was always "punctual and indefatigable," but in Congress he spent "a great part of his time fast asleep in his chair," to John Adams' dismay. His indolence "will prevent any thorough reformation of anything, and his"—"cunning" was the word Adams wanted and wrote but hardly dared use; he crossed it out—"and his silence and reserve render it very difficult to do anything with him." Occasionally, though, when politics was not involved, Franklin could be garrulous, as Adams knew from a night when the two shared a bed in a small tavern. Before blowing out the candle Adams closed the bedroom window.

"Oh!," said Franklin, "don't shut the window. We shall be suffocated."

Adams said he feared "the evening air."

"The air within this chamber will soon be, and indeed is now worse than that without doors," Franklin said. "Come! Open the window and come to bed, and I will convince you. I believe you are not acquainted with my theory of colds."

Adams opened the window and leaped into bed, saying that he had so much curiosity to hear his reasons that he would run the risk of a cold. Thereupon, Franklin "began an harangue upon air and cold and respiration and perspiration, with which I was so much amused that I soon fell asleep and left him and his philosophy together."

What manner of man was this sometimes garrulous, more often silent, old gentleman?

A genius? "His understanding is good enough for common uses, but not good enough for uncommon ones," said Thomas Jefferson, who liked and admired him. "He has very moderate abilities. He knows nothing of philosophy, but his few experiments in electricity," said John Adams, who developed an intense dislike for him.

Dispassionate? "I always knew him to be a very factious man," said the philosopher David Hume, a friend. "I am afraid that B.F., whose face at times turns white as the driven snow, with the extremes of wrath, may assert facts not true," said a friend who later became an enemy.

Virtuous? The most "hypocritical old rascal that ever existed —a man who, if ever one goes to hell, he will," said Lord Hillsborough, an enemy who had known him well in England. "I have a very high opinion of B.F.'s virtue and uncorrupted honesty," said another, "but party zeal throws down all the poles of truth and candor and lays all the soul waste to temptation without knowing or suspecting it."

Beloved? "I never really was much of an admirer of the doctor," remarked a citizen of Pennsylvania after listening to companions tear apart Franklin's character, "but I could hardly find it in my heart to paint the devil so bad." A once close friend, later an enemy, called him "a very artful, insinuating fellow, and very ready at expedients." John Dickinson, who headed the Pennsylvania delegation when Franklin arrived in Congress, hated him so much he refused to have a lightning rod on his city mansion, an obstinacy later paid for when lightning struck the house.

Congress for several months treated its world-famous sage circumspectly. Gradually, it dawned upon the delegates that any mission where wit, intelligence, and diplomacy might be of use must involve Franklin, and he, in turn, no matter how arduous the assignment, accepted it. In October 1775 he traveled up to Cambridge with Lynch and Harrison to confer with Washington about the siege of Boston. In March 1776, before the snows had cleared from the ground and traveling remained tortuous, Franklin with Charles Carroll and Carroll's cousin Father John Carroll trekked up to Canada seeking to cajole the citizens there to join the American cause. He returned from that ordeal in May, not only weary but in blinding pain from one of his recurring bouts with the gout. He spent the month of June recuperating on a friend's farm not far from the city. Jefferson sent his draft of the Declaration out to the farm on June 21. Franklin made only a few minor changes in the paper. He was well enough—or pretended to be—to attend Congress on July 2 to vote for independence, then stay on to watch the editing of the Declaration.

I have made it a rule," Franklin said to Jefferson, as the young man writhed in his seat, "whenever in my power, to avoid becoming a draughtsman of papers to be reviewed by a public body. I took my lesson from an incident which I will relate to you."

When I was a journeyman printer one of my companions, an apprentice hatter, having served out his time, was about to open shop for himself. His first concern was to have a handsome signboard, with a proper inscription. He composed it in these words:

JOHN THOMPSON, HATTER
MAKES AND SELLS HATS FOR READY MONEY

with a figure of a hat subjoined. But he thought he would submit it to his friends for their amendments. The

first he showed it to thought the word "hatter"
tautologous, because followed by the words "makes hats"
which show he was a hatter. It was struck out. The next
observed that the word "makes" might as well be
omitted, because the customers would not care who
made the hats. If good and to their mind, they would
buy, by whomever made. He struck it out. A third said
he thought the words "for ready money" were useless, as
it was not the custom of the place to sell on credit.
Everyone who purchased expected to pay. They were
parted with, and the inscription now stood:

JOHN THOMPSON
SELLS HATS

"*Sells* hats" says his next friend. "Why, nobody will
expect you to give them away. What then is the use of
that word?" It was stricken out, and "hats" followed it,
the rather, as there was one painted on the board. So his
inscription was reduced ultimately to

JOHN THOMPSON

with the figure of a hat subjoined."

Despite John Dickinson's heated objections to the Declaration,
it looked at first as though the paper would survive better than
John Thompson's sign. The opening paragraphs slid through with
only a few minor changes. So, too, did the first fifteen of the
charges against the king. The slight editing carried out here
sought only to increase the accuracy of the charge. For instance,
"He has suffered the administration of justice totally to cease in
some of these states. . . ." became "he has obstructed the administration of justice . . . ," for it could be argued that the king had
not closed the courts nor had the administration of justice "totally" ceased. In another charge Jefferson censured the standing
armies and ships of war sent to America during peace time.
Congress accepted the objection against standing armies, but
ships of war protected America's shores and trade; that part of the
charge was dropped. Only in the sixteenth charge did Congress

finally feel the need to shore up Jefferson's prose. That charge dealt with the use of foreign troops. To underscore the cruelty and perfidy of this act they added—their additions are in italics—that it was *"scarcely paralleled in the most barbarous ages and totally* unworthy of the head of a civilized nation."

Congress had now covered over half the Declaration. The minor alterations made thus far should have bothered Jefferson little. The easy sailing ended when the delegates reached the last of his charges, that dealing with slavery. The entire paragraph was thrown out. It went out, Jefferson said bitterly, "in complaisance to South Carolina and Georgia, who had never attempted to restrain the importation of slaves, and who on the contrary still wished to continue it. Our Northern brethren also, I believe, felt a little tender under those censures; for tho' their people have very few slaves themselves, yet they had been pretty considerable carriers of them to others." He might have added that most of the Northern delegates also owned or had owned slaves—Benjamin Franklin among them—and were equally embarrassed by Jefferson's paragraph.

The misery had only begun for Jefferson. Nearly every line of the concluding paragraphs was assailed by someone in the room. Earlier Jefferson had attacked George III in his capacity as king. When, however, at the start of the concluding section he wrote that

future ages will scarce believe that the hardiness of one man, adventured within the short compass of twelve years only, to build a foundation, so broad & undisguised, for tyranny over a people fostered & fixed in principles of freedom

he censured George as an individual. John Adams thought the attack "too personal, for I never believed George to be a tyrant in disposition and in nature," and Congress agreed with him. The passage was struck out.

The run of criticisms continued. Out went the obviously

untrue statement that all who had migrated to America had been "unassisted by the wealth or the strength of Great Britain." Congress also deleted the judgment that "submission to their parliament was no part of our constitution, nor ever in idea, if history may be credited," for there were too many instances in the past of America's accepting Parliamentary jurisdiction without complaint. Then came the most agonizing blow: Congress rejected all of the last half of Jefferson's first concluding paragraph, which dealt mainly with those "unfeeling brethren," the English people. The decision swept away some of Jefferson's happiest phrases— "the road to happiness & glory is open to us too; we will climb it apart from them"—but there were sound reasons for the cut. America was breaking its ties with Great Britain not because of the iniquities of the British people, but because of the king's crimes against America.

The final paragraph was reworked to include the original wording of Lee's resolution of June 7. Several of the delegates felt Jefferson had been remiss in his references to God. Two more were added to the last paragraph. One appealed "to the supreme judge of the world for the rectitude of our intentions." The other went into Jefferson's final sentence:

And for the support of this declaration *with a firm reliance on the protection of divine providence,* we mutually pledge to each other our lives, our fortunes, & our sacred honor.

Congress completed its revision of the Declaration in the early evening of July 4. What had the delegates achieved during the two and a half days spent on Jefferson's paper? They had, in spite of some forty additions and extensive cuts that reduced the length by one-quarter, left the document pretty much intact, especially that part of it that would appeal to future generations. Jefferson said years later that the Declaration's "authority rests . . . on the harmonizing sentiments of the day," and as far as pointing up those sentiments went, Congress improved his paper at every point. It eliminated any remark that tended to divide America—out went the diatribe against slavery, which especially angered the South, and along with it a reference to Scotch mercenaries, which jarred the sensibilities of an ethnic group —and added what it could to strengthen the union, as, for example, the reference to God which sought to satisfy the devout of the nation that the Revolution was being carried out under divine guidance.

The process of making Jefferson's Declaration into an American Declaration did more than improve the paper. It revealed that, despite strong divisive forces within the new nation, there appeared to exist a solid ideological basis for unity. Thirteen states, whose representatives only two years earlier had first met in Philadelphia and been appalled at the diversity of customs, laws, and traditions among the colonies, and who only three weeks earlier had been at loggerheads over the practical question of independence, had with little difficulty been able to agree on a set of fundamental political beliefs.

The thirteen clocks had been timed to strike as one, and also to strike the same tone. This, as the delegates knew, was remarkable and perhaps the most notable aspect of the Declaration of Independence as it left Congress. There may have been much in Jefferson's paper that dissatisfied or perturbed the delegates. Quite likely they voiced their complaints to the end, but when it seemed apparent that this was the best that could be produced to satisfy thirteen distinctly various colonies, defeat was accepted with the same grace, in the same spirit of realistic compromise, with which it had been accepted when independence itself, horrifying as it was to many of the delegates, became inevitable.

Jefferson and Congress, then, could be equally pleased with their joint handiwork. Now, the delegates might begin to ask themselves, how would America, and the world, too, for that matter, react to what John Dickinson had called "this skiff made of paper"? "We are now, sir," one member of Congress wrote on the morning of July 4, "embarked on a most tempestuous sea; life very uncertain, deceiving danger scattered thick around us, plots against the military, and it is whispered against the Senate. Let us prepare for the worst, we can die but once."

12

The Signing

The official printer placed July 4 at the top of his broadside
of the Declaration and thus accidentally that day came to
be celebrated with the pomp and ceremony John Adams
expected to be given over to July 2, the day Congress declared independence. John Hancock informed General
Washington of the decision in a brief note extraordinarily
appropriate to the moment:

6 July 1776

Sir:

The Congress for some time past, have had their attention occupied by one of the most interesting and important
subjects that could possibly come before them; or any other
assembly of men.

Altho' it is not possible to forsee the consequences of
human actions, yet it is nevertheless a duty we owe ourselves
and posterity, in all our public counsels, to decide in the best
manner we are able, and to leave the event to that Being
who controls both causes and events to bring about His own
determination.

Impressed with this sentiment, and at the same time fully convinced that our affairs may take a more favorable turn the Congress have judged it necessary to dissolve the connection between Great Britain and the American colonies, and to declare them free and independent states; as you will perceive by the enclosed Declaration, which I am directed to transmit to you, and to request you will have it proclaimed at the head of the army in the way you shall think most proper.

The first public celebration of independence occurred on July 8 when from the steps of the State House—eventually to be called Independence Hall—the Declaration was read aloud "in the presence of a great concourse of people." The crowd gave three huzzas, shouting with each, "God bless the Free States of North America!" A group of selected soldiers stepped up to rip down the king's arms from over the entrance to the State House and carried them over to the London Coffee House. In the afternoon, the city's five battalions paraded on the city commons "and gave us," said John Adams, "the *feu de joie*, notwithstanding the scarcity of powder." The sound of clanging bells filled the cool evening air—"the bells rang all day and almost all night"—and bonfires flickered throughout the city. The high point of the celebration came in the evening at the coffee house. There, as the great crowd cheered, the king's arms were heaved onto a mound of flaming wooden casks and the symbol of royal authority in Philadelphia swiftly vanished in fire and smoke.

"We have lived to see a period which a few years ago no human forecast could have imagined," a delegate wrote home, and then went on to temper his joy. "We have lived to see these colonies shake off, or rather declare themselves independent of a state which they once gloried to call their parent—I said *declare* themselves independent, for it is one thing for colonies to declare themselves independent and another to establish themselves in independence."

Soon after the bonfire at the London Coffee House the weary delegates began to give thought to a holiday at home. Congress still had too much work ahead—there was a confederation to form and a constitution to make for the new nation; ways must be found to supply Washington's army for the coming summer campaign; foreign nations must be solicited to help the fragile new nation stay alive— to adjourn for the summer, but one by one the delegates slipped away for a rest.

The first to go—but only for a short trip across the Delaware to visit his mother in New Jersey—was Joseph Hewes. "I had the weight of North Carolina on my shoulders within a day or two of three months; the service was too severe," he wrote the day the king's arms were burned. "My health was bad; such close attention made it worse; I nevertheless obstinately persisted in doing my duty to the best of my judgment and abilities and attended Congress the whole time, one day only excepted. This I did contrary to the repeated solicitations of my friends, some of whom I believe thought I should not be able to keep soul and body together till this time. Duty, inclination and self-preservation call on me now to make a little excursion in the country to see my mother. This is a duty which I have not allowed myself to perform during almost nine months that I have been here."

John Adams gave a more vivid account of what the battle for independence had done to him. "My face has grown pale," he wrote soon after the victory, "my eyes weak and inflamed, my nerves tremulous, and my mind weak as water —feverous heats by days and sweats by night are returned upon me, which is an infallible symptom with me that it is time to throw off all care, for a time, and take a little rest. I have several times, with the blessing of God, saved my life in this way, and am now determined to attempt it once more." (John Adams survived. Although he continued to grumble about his weak constitution, he had close to a half century of life still ahead of him.)

Samuel Adams should have been the first to depart for a vacation—he had not been home for over ten months—but there was too much unfinished business that he dare not trust to others. John Adams, though he had had a two-month holiday the previous winter, stood next in line, but the prize went to the newest and younger member of the delegation. "My deserving friend, Mr. Gerry, sets off tomorrow for Boston," John Adams wrote on July 15, "worn out of health by the fatigues of this station. He is an excellent man, and an active statesman. I hope he will soon return hither. I am sure I should be glad to go with him, but I cannot. I must write to have the guard relieved."

Elbridge Gerry
AGE: 32   MERCHANT

John Adams entrusted Gerry with a canister of tea to be delivered to his wife Abigail. He alerted her that a gift of leaves rarer than gold was on the way. But Gerry, he warned, "is an old bachelor, and what is worse a politician, and what is worse still a kind of soldier, so that I suppose he will have so much curiosity to see armies and fortifications and assemblies that you will lose many a fine breakfast at a time when you want them most." Gerry not only dawdled along the road; he gave the tea to Mrs. Samuel Adams when he arrived in Boston and put John's wife to considerable embarrassment attempting to retrieve it. Adams forgave the remissness. His absent-minded friend was "a man of immense worth," he said. "If every man here was a Gerry, the liberties of America would be safe against the gates of earth and hell."

Others felt differently. A fisher "in *troubled waters,*" said a less enthusiastic colleague, one of those men who "will prove eternal plagues to us." Even an admirer confessed that suspicion of other men's motives "was the weakest trait of his mind." He distrusted all those who held power and found it hard to distinguish between a George Washington and a George III. He suspected all who opposed him in debate, regardless of the issue, and his doubts about the good will of others in turn made his own proposals suspect. The acerbic Charles Thomson, permanent secretary of Congress, observed that Gerry "is of so peculiar a cast of mind that his pleasure seems proportioned to the absurdity of his schemes and who is only mortified when reason and common sense prevail."

As an Anglican reared in the land of Congregationalism, Gerry never expected a career in politics, and as a successful merchant satisfied with his lot had not desired one. He came from Marblehead, "a dirty, irregular, stinking place" that thrived on its fishing fleet. His father, a former English sea captain, had married a Boston girl and settled in Marblehead as a merchant, shipping out dried and salted fish in his vessels and importing wine, raisins, salt, and other items from Spain and the West Indies. He prospered enough to rear a family of twelve in comfortable circumstances and to send Gerry, his third son but the first to go to college, to Harvard, class of 1762. Gerry planned to become a physician but after graduation joined his father and brothers in the family business. In the decade that followed he did very well. The pinch of British taxes and trade restrictions slowly carried him into politics, and in 1772 Marblehead sent him to the provincial legislature. There he met and was wooed by Samuel Adams, who had already enticed John Hancock, another well-off bachelor, into his crusade against Britain. Back in Marblehead Gerry corresponded steadily with Adams. Gerry railed constantly in his letters against the "system of tyranny" England sought to impose on the colonies. When Adams called for a committee of correspondence to be erected in Marblehead, Gerry formed one with his father and a brother.

John Adams and John Hancock, at different times and each for his own reasons, abandoned Samuel Adams and his cause, only to be seduced back into the fold by the adept "old deluder." Gerry's moment for disillusion came in 1773. In the autumn of that year smallpox struck Marblehead. Gerry and his friends paid for the building of a hospital on the edge of town where those who had been inoculated could recover without the danger of infecting their families. In some way the people became convinced the hospital promoted rather than prevented the spread of the disease; they burned the building to the ground. The transformation of the people into a "savage mobility" stunned Gerry, and in January 1774, only a few weeks after the Boston Tea Party, he abandoned politics. Samuel Adams explained to him the difference between "a lawless attack on property" and "the people's rising in the defense of their liberties, and deliberately, and I may say rationally, destroying property." Gerry failed to catch the distinction.

Adams used the Boston Port Act to draw his malcontent disciple back into the movement. With Boston closed to shipping by the act, Marblehead became the most convenient port for funneling in the food and clothing being sent from other colonies. Adams asked Gerry to supervise the relief operation. Gerry performed superbly, and while he poured supplies into beleaguered Boston he was unwittingly lured back into public life, first as a member of the provincial convention, then, because of his administrative talents, as a member of the committee of safety, which would direct Massachusetts' armed resistance against Britain. Though little known outside the colony, he had become so important within it that the British would have been happy to capture him the night they marched toward Lexington. As it was, they almost did, forcing him to flee in his nightgown to the safety of a cornfield that April evening. Through the rest of 1775, while Hancock and the Adamses were in Philadelphia, Gerry wore himself out organizing the resistance in Massachusetts—rounding up ammunition and supplies for the army, supervising the erection of forts, marshaling troops, food, clothing, and whatever else was needed as the demand arose. None of his work was motivated by an affection for the people, of whom he still remained suspicious. "They now feel rather too much their own impatience," he said, "and it requires great skill to produce such subordination as is necessary."

Late in the year the word went out that Samuel Adams wanted

Thomas Cushing dropped from the Massachusetts delegation in Congress and replaced by Gerry. Cushing was known to be luke-warm for independence, while Gerry supported it vigorously. "New England will not be satisfied with less," he said, "since not only the government but the people of Great Britain are corrupt and destitute of public virtue." Gerry arrived in Congress early in February 1776. He did not make a good first impression. A colleague who liked him found him "slow in his perceptions and in his manner of doing business, and stammering in his speech." But eight days after arriving Congress placed him on what would later be called the treasury board, and his performance there, where he could display his administrative skill, won respect. He was admired, too, for making the country's welfare his own, even when it worked against his interests. He routed his ships to ports that could best provide supplies to fight the war. He pushed for price controls to keep down profiteering when most merchants opposed them. But his indelible doubts about the integrity of all those who differed from him stamped him a man difficult to live with. "He knew and embraced truth when he saw it," a friend said, but he embraced it too resolutely, as a vision handed down from above rather than something perceived by a fallible man.

After casting his vote for independence and setting out for home carrying John Adams' canister of tea in his bag, a worry began to plague Gerry, and soon after passing through New York City he sent back a note addressed to both Adamses. "Pray subscribe for me the Declaration of Independence, if the same is to be signed as proposed," he wrote. "I think we ought to have the privilege when necessarily absent of voting and signing by proxy." A space was left on the embossed copy of the Declaration, and Elbridge Gerry filled it with his signature when he returned to Congress in September.

On July 19, upon learning that New York would allow its delegation to sign, Congress ordered the Declaration to be engrossed, with the title altered from "A Declaration by the Representatives of the United States of America" to "The

Unanimous Declaration of the Thirteen United States of America." On August 2 the delegates paused in the business of the day in order that all those present might sign the engrossed copy.

Facts about the signing are few; anecdotes abound. Hancock, after centering his name below the text, is supposed to have said: "There! John Bull can read my name without spectacles, and may now double his reward of £500 for my head. *That* is my defiance." He is also supposed to have said: "We must be unanimous. There must be no pulling different ways; we must all hang together." To that remark Benjamin Franklin is supposed to have replied: "Yes, we must all hang together, or most assuredly we shall all hang separately." Stephen Hopkins, who was afflicted with palsy, is supposed to have said when his turn came: "My hand trembles, but my heart does not!"

These and numerous other tales of the signing that survive may be true, but all came into circulation long after the event and none has been verified by a corroborating source. The most circumstantial account of the occasion comes from Benjamin Rush, who included it in a letter to John Adams in 1811. Rush recalled of that day "the pensive and awful silence which pervaded the house when we were called up, one after another, to the table of the President of Congress to subscribe what was believed by many at that time to be our own death warrants." William Ellery of Rhode Island stood at the table beside Secretary Charles Thomson to watch the face of each delegate as he wrote his name.

William Ellery
AGE: 48   LAWYER

Mr. Ellery, who lived to be ninety-two, paced himself for a long life. "He was not fond of bodily activity," an acquaintance said, "and always walked with a regular measured step, as if he were

consulting his ease as far as he could in doing a thing for which
he had small relish." He rode as he walked, slowly, and while
colleagues ruminated on profounder matters Mr. Ellery, especially on the long journey between Newport and Philadelphia,
gave attention to the trivia of life, such as:

Petticoat Government: The black man who engaged to attend
me on the journey fell sick or pretended to be so. . . . [He] was
a married man and alas and lack-a-day was under petticoat government, and his sovereign wanted to keep him at home to wait upon
her. If I had known previously to my engaging him that he had
been under this kind of domination, I should have consulted his
domina and procured her consent before I had depended upon
him, and not suffered this sad disappointment. Well—let the
ambitious say what they please, women have more to do with the
government of this world than they are willing to allow. Oh! Eve,
Eve!

Bedbugs: I surveyed my bed according to custom before I
ventured to enter it (search first before you enter is no bad rule)
and lo! a bug of enormous size displayed his huge brown bloated
corpse. I instantly applied the blaze of the candle to him and with
many sincere imprecations offered him a burnt sacrifice to the
Goddess of Impurity.

Man with a wig: A little diverting affair took place here [near
Paramus, New Jersey]. The children who had never before seen
a gentleman with a wig on were, it seems, not a little puzzled by
my friend's headdress. They thought it was his natural hair, but
it differed so much from mine and theirs in its shape that they
did not know what to make of it. . . . It is not a little remarkable
that children who had lived on a public road should have never
before seen a wig.

Suffering Man: The Devil had smote [Job] from the sole of
his foot unto the crown of his head, whereas I was afflicted
but in the middle region. But then I was attacked *a posteriori*
and in a spot the most exposed in riding to injury of any in
the human body. [A physician gave me] an *emplastrum* of
diachylon cum gummis. And I am almost well. Into whose
hands this journal may fall I know not, but humanity bids me
tell the reader if ever he should be in my situation not to forget *diachylon cum gummis.*

Ellery arrived in Congress May 14, 1776, a replacement for Samuel Ward, an old political ally who had died in March. His Rhode Island colleague, Stephen Hopkins, sent word home he was "pleased with the gentleman you have appointed," though they had once been enemies. Ellery performed well on committees but rarely spoke in Congress, preferring to amuse "himself in writing epigrams on the speakers which were generally witty and pertinent and sometimes political." One colleague judged him "somewhat cynical in his temper." Ellery would have smiled at that. While a student at Harvard, class of 1747, he had boarded with a family firmly ruled over by an elderly judge. Once at the dinner table when "I was letting out a stream of my fluent nonsense," the old man looked up from his plate and said, "Young man, bridle your tongue, or you will get the name of a humorist."

As a young man Ellery showed no inclination to follow his father, deputy governor of Rhode Island, into politics, and his father expressed no desire to bring him into the family mercantile firm in Newport. After graduation he hung around Harvard for a year, drifted down to Newport for a while, then back to Cambridge where he picked up a master of arts degree and married a girl whose "blooming countenance" had charmed him at the boarding house table. He earned enough at odd jobs to rear a large family—when his wife died after fourteen years of marriage she left behind six children, and a second wife gave him five more—but twenty years passed before he settled into law for a career. "If the year before I graduated I had determined upon law, or physic, especially the latter, I am persuaded that I should have led a more profitable and useful life," he recalled. "But no one advised me, and I made no choice. I entered into small commerce without a spirit of enterprise or skill in trade; that would not do; I had married a wife, and could not submit to be an understrapper to a physician. I became a clerk of a court; there I copied writs and declarations, gained some knowledge of practice, and stood forth a dabbler . . . a quack lawyer."

He also dabbled in politics along the way, an ally of Governor Ward during the long feud with Hopkins. Brashness led to the scare of his life during the Stamp Act crisis. He thought it would be great fun to drum up a mob to protest the parliamentary tax. The mob, stroked on rum provided by Ellery, made a riotous march through town, threatening the property of leading citizens, that of Ellery's among others. The stamp agent, whose effigy Ellery had caused to be burned earlier in the evening, came out of hiding and with great courage restored order. Ellery behaved more circumspectly thereafter but with no less ardor. "You must exert yourself. To be ruled by Tories, when we may be ruled by Sons of Liberty—how debasing," he said as the Second Congress was assembling. "You must rouse up all that is Roman in Providence. There is liberty and fire enough; it only requires the application of the bellows. Blow, then, a blast that will shake the country."

In Congress he kept his voice muted, leaving it to older hands to carry the weight of the great debate for independence. The only time known when he stepped out of the background was the day of the signing, when he stood beside Secretary Thomson's table. Only once, as Benjamin Rush remembered it, did anyone break "the pensive and awful silence" and then it was to crack a joke at Ellery's expense. Benjamin Harrison, glancing from his large paunch to William Ellery's thin frame said, "I shall have a great advantage over you, Mr. Ellery, when we are all hung for what we are now doing. From the size and weight of my body I shall die in a few minutes, but from the lightness of your body you will dance in the air an hour or two before you are dead." As Rush recollected, "this speech procured a transient smile, but it was soon succeeded by the solemnity with which the whole business was conducted."*

---

*An historical puzzle enters here. In recalling this scene years later Rush said Harrison directed his comment to Elbridge Gerry. Gerry later substantiated the episode. But the evidence is irrefutable that Gerry was

Later, Ellery said that all who stepped up to the table that morning showed only "undaunted emotion."

All the doubters—Robert Morris, George Read, and William Hooper—and the two possible doubters—Carter Braxton and Thomas Lynch, Jr.—signed on August 2. A number of those who signed were new to Congress and had not been present a month earlier to vote for independence. There were five new faces in the Pennsylvania delegation—Benjamin Rush, George Clymer, James Smith, George Taylor, and George Ross. Samuel Chase had returned from Maryland bringing with him Charles Carroll of Carrollton, reputedly the richest man in America.

Charles Carroll of Carrollton
AGE: 39   COUNTRY GENTLEMAN

Only two men in Congress could, if they wished, boast they had envisioned independence for America long before anybody else. One was John Adams. "If we can remove the turbulent Gallicks," he predicted in 1755, "the only way to keep us from setting up for ourselves is to disunite us." The other was Charles Carroll, the single Roman Catholic to sign the Declaration. In 1763 he wrote from London telling his father not to worry that he would abandon his homeland for the love of an English girl. "I cannot sacrifice the future aggrandizement of our family to a woman," he said; "America is a growing country; in time it will and must be independent."

Carroll was a small man physically. Everything else about him —his wealth, his spirit, his intelligence—was outsized. His for-

---

not present the day of the signing. I have assumed that after the passage of thirty-five years Rush confused "Elbridge" with "Ellery," admittedly a shaky assumption that does not explain why Gerry "acquiesced in the correctness of B. Harrison's speech to him."

tune, which the gossip in Congress "computed to be worth two hundred thousand pounds sterling," was said to be the largest in America. He was a stranger to intrigue. When he heard from a fellow Catholic, General Thomas Conway, disparaging talk about George Washington's leadership, he said flatly that "anybody that displeased or did not admire the commander in chief ought not to be kept in the army." Conway did not like this unequivocal view. "Mr. Carroll might be a good Papist," he said, "but I am sure the sentiments he expresses are neither Roman or Catholic." John Adams did not know whether to praise more Carroll's talents —"his abilities are very good, his knowledge and learning extensive"—or his spirit. "In the cause of American liberty," he told a friend, "his zeal, fortitude, and perseverance have been so conspicuous that he is said to be marked out for peculiar vengeance by the friends of administration." The man had only one large flaw: a low regard for Congress. "We murder time, and chat it away in idle, impertinent talk," he said. Members are too "fond of talking, and not much addicted to thinking." He seldom spoke from the floor, choosing to remain "a silent hearer of such speeches as neither edified, entertained, or instructed me."

Carroll was born at Annapolis, Maryland, educated by Jesuits until he was eleven, then spent the next seventeen years completing his education abroad, principally in France and England. When he returned home the year of the Stamp Act his father turned over Carrollton Manor to him, a ten-thousand-acre plantation in Frederick County. He adopted the signature Charles Carroll of Carrollton to distinguish himself from the other Charleses in the sprawling Carroll family. He took no part in public affairs for several years—Catholics were barred in Maryland from holding public office—but satisfied himself with managing his plantation and, after marrying a cousin, rearing a family. He did, though, establish friendly ties with those in the colony leading the opposition against Britain, notably Samuel Chase.

"Carroll, we have the better of our opponents—we have completely written them down," Chase told him some time after all the Townshend duties but that on tea had been repealed.

"And do you think," Carroll asked, "that writing will settle the question between us?"

"To be sure," said Chase. "What else can we resort to?"

"The bayonet," Carroll said. "Our arguments will only raise the feelings of the people to that pitch when open war will be looked to as the arbiter of the dispute."

Months before the British marched on Lexington Carroll predicted that if war came America would win it. "If we are beaten on the plains, we will retreat to our mountains and defy them," he told a friend in England who had said it would take no more than six thousand British regulars to crush the colonies. It may take years but eventually "your armies will evacuate our soil, and your country retire, an immense loser, from the contest.—No, sir —we have made up our minds to abide the issue of the approaching struggle, and though much blood may be spilt, we have no doubt of our ultimate success."

Active participation in the Revolution began for Carroll in 1774 with election to the provincial convention, the committee of correspondence, and the committee of safety. In February 1776 Congress chose him—though not yet a member, he was America's most eminent Catholic layman and spoke fluent French—along with his cousin, Father John Carroll, to accompany Franklin and Chase on a mission to Canada to allay French suspicions of Protestant America. When Carroll returned from the abortive trip in the late spring, he found the Maryland convention dominated by a bloc of members who refused to let the colony's delegation in Congress vote for independence. Carroll had a large hand in convincing the convention it was too late to hope for reconciliation. The instructions were changed to permit Maryland's representatives to favor independence. On July 4, 1776, Carroll was chosen by the convention to join the delegation in Congress. The day he took his seat there, July 18, he was honored by his new colleagues with election to one of the most important standing committees, the board of war and ordnance. Two weeks later, as Charles Carroll of Carrollton stepped up to sign the

Declaration, someone in the room is supposed to have remarked: "There go millions."

There was also a new face in the Connecticut delegation,
the dour and humorless William Williams.

William Williams
AGE: 45   MERCHANT

Like Samuel Adams, Williams had been bred for the church but
shifted to politics. He, too, regarded the Revolution as a crusade,
and early wondered if America had virtue enough "to take up
arms and shed rivers of blood in defense of our almost infinitely
important cause." After Lexington he gave his life to the cause.
He closed his business and exchanged all the hard cash in the till
for continental currency. In a stream of speeches and essays he
cajoled and exhorted the people of Connecticut to the banner.
Until victory came, he said, no man had the right to put personal
interests first. When he heard that a Connecticut colonel sharing
in the siege of Boston had left his post upon learning Washington,
a Southerner, had been appointed commander in chief, Williams
hurried to Boston and coaxed the colonel back to duty. Even a
slight relaxing of the vigil angered him. When the people of
Philadelphia paused to celebrate the first anniversary of independence, he reported with disgust that "a great expenditure of
liquor, powder, etc., took up the day, and of candles thro' the city
a good part of the night."

No man gave more of himself to the Revolution, and none with
a lifetime in politics achieved less in Congress. A warm temper
reduced his effectiveness. "He possessed," said an acquaintance,
"during the whole of his life, a redundancy of spirit and vehe-
mence of expression, which frequently created in himself strong
and sorrowful feelings." But others in Congress had high tempers.
Williams failed because he could not escape from his New England upbringing. "There are strange mortals in Congress, be

assured," he remarked one day. " 'Tis hard to say what some of them aim at, but easy to say a number invariably hate and persecute every New England man and can embroil matters exceedingly." He particularly distrusted the people of Pennsylvania, who contested Connecticut's God-given right to occupy the Wyoming Valley, a fertile stretch of land claimed by "the overgrown, overlanded Mr. Penn." They "have a fixed hatred of New England and everything that belongs to it but money," he said, "and that is all the God they worship." Not surprisingly, a Pennsylvania delegate dismissed Williams as "a well meaning weak man, often misled by state prejudices." He embarrassed even colleagues within his delegation. Four months after signing the Declaration he left for home saying he doubted he could "do any good if he stayed." Oliver Wolcott, who had watched him finagle to fill every vacant continental post with friends and relatives, said "the true reason of his return was that he did not know of any particular personal or family interest to induce him to tarry longer."

Williams knew after the months in Philadelphia he could be happy only in New England, happier when within the borders of Connecticut, and happiest when back in Lebanon, the town where he was born and reared and lived out his life. The religious ardor he brought to the war against Britain- "the step-mother country" he called her after the attempt to impose taxes on beloved Connecticut—owed something to his upbringing by a devout Congregational minister and something to a short tour of duty during the French and Indian War. He went to Harvard, class of 1754, expecting to follow his father into the clergy, but after a postgraduate course at home in theology, he saw God had not called him into the church. During the French and Indian War he enlisted as a surgeon with a company bound for Lake George. Robert Treat Paine, there at the same time as a spurious chaplain, came away with a terrible head cold, while Williams returned home "disgusted with the British commanders," according to family tradition. "Their haughtiness and arbitrary conduct and their inattention to the interests of America made a powerful and lasting impression upon his mind."

Williams had an aptitude for "mechanical pursuits," a fondness for mathematics and the classics; architecture especially fascinated him. But none of these interests offered a livelihood. He opened a store in Lebanon and prospered. An appointment as justice of the peace and election to the provincial assembly carried him into politics, and from then on that pursuit and business absorbed his time. At the age of forty he paused to marry the daughter of Governor Jonathan Trumbull. The alliance made him part of the oligarchy that dominated Connecticut politics, and three years later he assumed the second most powerful office in the colony, speaker of the legislature.

Williams' religious fervor colored his rhetoric. After Parliament closed the port of Boston to all shipping, he dispatched shipments of food and clothing there "for the relief of your poor" and reassured friends that "the principles we maintain are founded in eternal truth and justice, and they must and will prevail." After the British marched on Lexington all who opposed the cause became "enemies of God and man." No one perceived more quickly than he that Americans were now embarked on a mission "unspeakably important and big with the fate of born and unborn millions." That cause had nothing to do with revolution or democracy. He continued, as in the past, to deplore "an unlawful assembly (or mob, if you please)," and to hold that a politician should vote as his conscience and experience directed him, not as the people wished. Once the land had been purged of British corruptions all would be well with America.

After the fighting at Lexington broke out, Williams allowed himself only a few hours sleep each night. While shuttling between duties as speaker of the house and clerk to the council of safety, he spurred the citizens of Lebanon to contribute all they could spare to the war. When the colony chose him to attend the Second Congress, he begged off the assignment. There was too much for him to do in Connecticut. Only pleas for relief from colleagues who had endured extended tours in Philadelphia persuaded him to accept a share of the burden. "With great reluctance I set out for this place and reached it near the last of July, after the most sultry and fatiguing journey that I ever performed by much," he reported of his trip to Philadelphia.

He arrived too late to vote for independence but in time to sign the Declaration. "What will be the event of things God only knows," he wrote ten days after the signing. "The Judge of all the earth will do right. He has done great things for us. He will not yet forsake us, I believe, tho' most of us have forsaken Him. But I trust many, many thousands have not bowed the knee to Baal."

13

Arrivals and Departures

The departures for home picked up shortly after the signing. Benjamin Harrison and Carter Braxton were the first to go, along with Button Gwinnett. Neither Gwinnett nor Braxton ever returned to Congress.

Samuel Adams went next. "Between you and me, [he] is completely worn out," John Adams had reported back to Boston shortly after the vote for independence. "I wish he had gone home six months ago and rested himself. Then he might have done it without any disadvantage. But in plain English he has been so long here, and his strength, spirit, and abilities so exhausted that an hundred such delegates would not be worth a shilling." With his name leading the list of Massachusetts signatures on the Declaration, Samuel Adams could head for home at peace with himself. For years he had lived filled with fears—fear of the tyranny and oppression imposed by the sinful British upon innocent America, fear of a strong government ("he loved economy and simplicity in government"), fear of a standing army (the "shoeblacks of society," he called them). The list was end-less. Now that America had declared herself free and independent he had nothing left to fear. "This being done," he said, "things will go on in the right channel and our country will be saved."

Traveling with Samuel Adams back to New England was one of his and John Adams' closest friends in Congress, William Whipple of New Hampshire.

William Whipple
AGE: 46   MARINER-MERCHANT

A weather-beaten face and crusty manner led colleagues to call him the "old sea captain," though he was far from old, had not commanded a ship for fifteen years, and would end the war a general in charge of the New Hampshire militia. Neither soft words nor halfway measures sat well with Whipple. "I should be glad if their fellow citizens would assist them," he told a friend back home who had complained for the want of resolution among members of Congress, "so far as to cut the throats of a few of these pests to society who under the character of speculators are at this time doing more mischief than ever was done to a community by any set of villains since the creation." Talk of a compromise with Britain disgusted him. "War with all its horrors is preferable to an inglorious peace," he said. "I hope we shall never consent to such a peace as will involve posterity in greater evils than we have suffered."

Whipple was born and reared in the seafaring town of Kittery, Maine. In school he learned to read and write enough arithmetic to initiate him into the mysteries of navigation. He went to sea when still a youngster. By the age of twenty-one he had a ship of his own. The search for cargoes carried him into the slave trade. He bought a black for a servant, but later, influenced by compatriots' talk about the rights to liberty for all, freed him. In Congress he applauded a plan to raise "some black regiments" in the South.

"This will, I suppose, lay a foundation for the emancipation of those poor wretches in that country, and I hope be the means of dispensing the blessings of freedom to all the human race in America."

Some ten years of life at sea proved enough. When thirty years old, he married a girl from Portsmouth, New Hampshire, and settled down there as a merchant in partnership with his brother. Neither the Stamp Act nor other events in the ensuing decade drew him into politics. When he decided at last to act it was, typically, in no halfway manner. In 1775 he gave up his share in the firm of William & Joseph Whipple and got elected to the New Hampshire legislature. From that day on it outraged him to hear that men had to be persuaded to serve their country. "What can be the meaning of this?" he asked a friend. "Do gentlemen still think it hazardous to appear in a character that will render them obnoxious to the British tyrant? Or are they afraid their private interest will suffer?"

New Hampshire sent him to Congress in January 1776. John Adams sized him up at once as "another excellent member in principle and disposition, as well as understanding." Soon it was "my friend Whipple." Later, when each was searching for cheaper lodgings, they joined together in a boardinghouse that mutually satisfied them. The two differed on few things. Whipple's appraisal of the danger of a foreign alliance—"We must expect all nations will be influenced by their own interest and so far as we may expect the friendship of any power that inclines to form an alliance with us, but if we expect more we shall certainly be disappointed"—had the tart bite of Adams' own judgment. When friends back home complained about Congress' indecisiveness it could have been Adams (it happened to be Whipple) who wrote: Congressmen are "mere men you know—men that are subject to all the frailties and imperfections of human nature."

Congress put Whipple to work at once. His knowledge of business and the sea dictated seats on the marine and commerce committees. Other assignments followed. In May his colleagues chose him, such was their respect, for the committee to confer with Washington on military plans for the summer campaign. He was back in Congress in time to join in the debate on independence and to vote in favor of it. Later, when leaving Congress to take command of the militia in New Hampshire the sharp-tongued "old" gentlemen penned an affectionate note to his fellow-delegates—"those worthy patriots who first stepped forward, braved every danger, and combatted the greatest difficulties, and by their virtuous struggles, and unremitted exertions have thus far rescued the country from the hand of tyranny."

As the old hands moved out new ones, or old ones refreshed, flowed in. Richard Henry Lee returned in late August, followed shortly by George Wythe. Their return freed Thomas Jefferson to visit his ailing wife. Late in August Lewis Morris came over from New York, where he had been occupied in local politics and in shoring up defenses against an imminent British attack.

Lewis Morris

AGE: 50   COUNTRY GENTLEMAN

Congress knew what it lost only when the "cheerful, amiable" Lewis Morris gave up his seat after signing the Declaration to his half-brother Gouverneur Morris, who turned out to be "an eternal speaker," a man full of artifice, "and for brass equal to any I am acquainted with," according to one delegate. Lewis Morris, on the other hand, caused men to stumble when listing his virtues. He "possessed a lofty stature, a singularly handsome face, and the most graceful demeanor," said a breathless contemporary as he edged into the ornate statement, "with a temperament so enthusiastic and ardent, and a disposition so benevolent and generous, as to render him in his native province the universal favorite of his coevals." An Indian did better. "Brothers of the Thirteen Fires, I am glad to see you," Chief Cornplanter told Congress, when asking for a man to negotiate with his tribe. "We have long known General Morris and would be pleased you would appoint him. He is also a very good man, and much beloved by the Indians."

Morris' grandfather had been the first royal governor of New Jersey, but his father preferred farming to politics and spent his life running Morrisania, the estate he had inherited which lay north of Manhattan Island just across the Harlem River. Lewis Morris took after his father. After graduating from Yale, class of 1746, he married and then joined his father in managing Morrisania. The estate became his with the death of his father in 1762. Politics did not intrude on Morris' serene life as a country gentleman until 1769, when Britain's continuing determination to tax the colonies impelled him to stand for a seat in the provincial assembly. He won. His name surfaced in the news only occasionally during the next six years, but his resistance to British imperial policy never wavered. Few of his wealthy neighbors in Westchester County—a number of whom later became Loyalists —approved of his stand. In the spring of 1775 he headed the county's delegation to New York's first provincial convention and, as the leading Whig of his county, the convention chose him to attend the Second Congress.

Congress often revealed a deftness, a collective wisdom in the use of members' talents, it rarely received credit for. It shunted Morris to committees where his amiable personality and the practical knowledge of a man who had managed a large estate for years would do the most good. Through 1775 and 1776 he spent his time searching out ways to supply the army with tent cloth, shoes, and clothing, saltpeter, sulphur, and gunpowder. By luck or design he was chosen to visit Pittsburgh in the autumn of 1775 to negotiate a truce with western tribes. The success of that venture led to a seat on the committee dealing with Indian affairs. There he arranged for Thomas Paine, then, as so often, in need of money, to serve as a paid secretary to a delegation attending an Indian conference. In one of those curious alliances revolutions make, Morris, the landed gentleman, and Paine, the former maker of ladies' stays, became good friends. Later Morris watched over Paine's house and farm in New Rochelle while Paine was in Paris stoking up the fires of the French Revolution.

Early in June 1776 the New York convention appointed Morris general in command of the Westchester County militia. He left Congress to take up his new post as the great debate on independence got underway. A British invasion of New York was expected any day, but although a flotilla of troop ships hovered off the coast the enemy had not landed a man by the end of June. To fill up the empty days Morris joined the provincial convention instead of returning to Philadelphia. There he voted for a change in instructions that would allow the New York delegation in Congress to sign the Declaration. At the end of August, "General Morris suggested sundry reasons to the convention for his attendance at Philadelphia"—no doubt one being a desire to sign the Declaration.

Family tradition has it that when he was about to sign he was warned that to do so risked the lost of his property to the British, whose troops were then within gunshot of Morrisania. "Damn the consequences, give me the pen," Morris is said to have replied. He soon paid for his rashness with the despoliation of Morrisania. He endured the loss, an admiring friend said, "without repining."

Stephen Hopkins lingered in Philadelphia until early September waiting for a replacement. When none had come by then, he turned Rhode Island's affairs over to William Ellery. He felt the weight of his sixty-nine years and thought it would be some time before he was strong enough to return to Congress. (He never did come back, though he remained active in New England politics throughout the Revolution.) "I should be exceedingly glad that Governor Hopkins might return," Ellery wrote after his departure, "for he is well acquainted with the mode of business and is well esteemed in Congress, and I have reason to think from what hath passed that we should act in concert and harmony." But if Hopkins felt too tired to come back, Ellery added, "it would be best that two should be immediately appointed, for matters of great consequence will be on the carpet."

In October, Wolcott came back from Connecticut and signed the Declaration. Caesar Rodney the same month left for Delaware full of bitterness. Only a few weeks after he had signed the Declaration the people of Delaware rejected him for a seat in the new state's constitutional convention, then about to convene. (Ironically, they endorsed George Read, who had voted against independence.) The fault was "your bad policy" Caesar told his brother Thomas, a neophyte to politics. The ticket had lost partly because Thomas Rodney had allowed a company of militia—all of whom were voters—"to march away just before the election." The defeat cut deeply, and a later one in November—he failed to be re-elected to his seat in Congress—even deeper. Rodney renounced politics. "I intend to leave the public and take the private paths of life—future generations will honor those names that are neglected by the present race." The mood soon passed. Rodney continued to live enmeshed in Delaware politics the rest of his life, which ended in 1784 when cancer carried him away.

In November, New Hampshire sent William Thornton, a man of good humor, to flesh out its delegation in Congress.

ꞔMatthew ꞔThornton
AGE: ABOUT 62   PHYSICIAN

"Funny as Tristram Shandy," said one colleague. "He has a large budget of droll stories, with which he entertains company perpetually." Large-boned and tall—over six feet—he wore an exceedingly grave countenance that rarely admitted a smile. "His posture, and manner of narrating, were as peculiar as the faculty itself," a contemporary said. "When he placed his elbows upon his knees, with his hands supporting his head, it was the signal for the *erectis auribus* of the assembly. Commencing with a slow articulation, and a solemn countenance, he gradually proceeded in his tale, casting, at intervals, his black and piercing eyes upon the countenances of his hearers, to detect the emotions excited in their breasts. . . . His ingenuity in this accomplishment was astonishing."

Thornton was born in northern Ireland. When he was four his father brought the family to America. They settled first in Maine, then near Worcester, Massachusetts. It was expected the boy would become a farmer, like everyone else in the back country. Thornton balked and apprenticed himself to a local physician. He completed his studies when twenty-six and moved to Londonberry, New Hampshire, an enclave of Scotch–Irish, and there began to practice. Five years later, still a bachelor, he signed on as an undersurgeon for the Fort Louisbourg expedition, which ended in the greatest military triumph Americans, on their own, had then achieved—capture of the great French fort at the mouth of the St. Lawrence River. Back home Thornton became a fixture in the local militia; eventually he rose to the rank of colonel. When he was forty-four, still a bachelor, Londonberry sent him to the provincial assembly. Two years later he at last married, late but in time to rear five children.

His career in politics moved along unremarkably until the Stamp Act. In the decade that followed virtually every political office available to a citizen of New Hampshire fell to him: president of the provincial congress, chairman of the committee of safety, speaker of the house, member of the council, president of the constitutional convention, associate justice of the superior court. Like most politicians, he revealed only as much of himself and his opinions as the moment called for. He attended church regularly, but as an acquaintance observed, "it is not ascertained that he ranked among any of the established sects of Christians." Once, however, a religious zealot who pressed hard drove his views on original sin into the open.

"Why," said Thornton, "I satisfy myself about it in this manner. Either original sin is divisible or indivisible. If it was divisible every descendant of Adam and Eve must have a part, and the share which falls to each individual at this day is so small a particle, that I think it is not worth considering. If indivisible, then the whole quantity must have descended in a right line, and must now be possessed by one person only, and the chances are millions and millions and millions to one that that person is now in Asia or Africa, and that I have nothing to do with it."

Toward money alone, "which in some degree detracted from the dignity of the character which he generally sustained," did Thornton have what might be called a religious attitude. He was, for a small-town physician, a comparatively wealthy man when he arrived in Philadelphia. "He was never known to be unjust," it was said in his defense, "although he rigidly enforced his rights, without reference to the smallness of the amount; hence he was considered severe in his pecuniary claims."

Thornton had nothing to do with the debates in Congress over independence. He was not chosen a delegate until September 12, 1776, and did not take his seat until November 3. When he arrived in Philadelphia he put up at a boarding house where Samuel Adams shared quarters with Roger Sherman and Jared Ingersoll of Connecticut—all solemn gentlemen. The mixture of personalities tickled John Adams. "Between the fun of Thornton and the gravity of Sherman, and the formal Toryism of Ingersoll, Adams will have a curious life of it," he said.

By now, signing the Declaration had come to be a loyalty oath to the new nation. According to Thomas McKean, the delegates had agreed "that no person should have a seat in Congress during [1776] until he should have signed the Declaration, in order (as I have been given to understand) to prevent traitors or spies from worming themselves amongst us." Thornton signed sometime in November.

The last to sign was Thomas McKean.

$\mathcal{T}$homas $\mathcal{M}$c$\mathcal{K}$ean

AGE: 42　POLITICIAN

The mystery of personality is here apparent. Less than a year separated McKean and his friend George Read in age. Both were reared Presbyterians, educated by the same Presbyterian clergyman, were admitted to the bar when twenty years old, practiced law in New Castle, Delaware, married the same year, and opposed the Stamp Act and other manifestations of British oppression that followed. Read fought independence and voted against it; McKean favored independence and voted for it.

Colleagues generally liked Read and respected his opinion whether or not they agreed with it. McKean aroused mixed feelings. "A man of talent," one delegate said, "of great vanity, extremely fond of power, and entirely governed by passions, ever pursuing the object present with warm enthusiastic zeal without much reflection or forecast." Privately, McKean confessed to favor government by the elite. "I shall only say that his conduct" in private, an acquaintance remarked, "gave no token of the zeal he not long afterwards displayed in the democratic career. But, as it is the people who make governors—*Eh! que faire Mons. Peltier?*—what the deuce is an eager candidate to do?" Once, though, McKean carelessly dropped his guard in public. The citizens of Pennsylvania, he said, are comprised one half of "traitors, Tories, apostate Whigs, and British agents," one half of "fools, geese, and clodhoppers."

McKean entered politics as a youngster, becoming deputy prothonotary of New Castle County when eighteen, and thereafter moving steadily from one public office to another: deputy attorney general, clerk of the provincial assembly, member of the assembly, judge of the court of common pleas, collector of customs for New Castle. As a judge during the Stamp Act crisis he rashly ordered his court to stay open and business to proceed as usual on unstamped paper. He attended the Stamp Act Congress with Rodney and spoke with accustomed warmth for firm resistance to British policy. Though wary of the mother country's designs on America, he cheerfully accepted the sinecure of customs collector when it was offered to him. Serving as one of the king's officers dampened his ardor for a time, but the crisis over tea revived it, and the closing of the port of Boston again set it afire. The provincial convention sent him to the First Congress. There he combined business with a honeymoon. On September 3 he married a woman from New Castle—his first wife had died the previous year, leaving McKean with six children; his second would give him four more—then two days later attended the opening session of Congress.

McKean came to the Second Congress saying he knew of "no right or authority in Parliament" to regulate American affairs in any way. Soon, although "almost wore down" by his congressional duties, he was agitating for independence. "I do think we shall lose our liberties, properties, and lives, too, if we do not take this step," he said. He warned the doubtful in Congress "that foreign mercenaries are coming to destroy us." In June 1776 he returned to Delaware and pried from the provincial convention permission for its delegation in Congress to vote for independence.

A few days after McKean had cast his vote for independence he left for New Jersey with a battalion of troops under his command. Months passed before he got around to signing the embossed copy of the Declaration. For some reason his name was not among the Signers when an abbreviated version of Congress' *Journal* was published in 1777. McKean took care to rectify the ommission. "Modesty should not rob any man of his just honor," he said, "when by that honor his modesty cannot be offended."

Epilogue

By February 1777, only six months after the signing, Congress was down to twenty-two delegates, and most of these were new faces. "I have the melancholy prospect before me of a Congress continually changing until very few faces remain that I saw in the First Congress," John Adams reported. "Not one from South Carolina, not one from North Carolina, only one from Virginia, only two from Maryland, not one from Pennsylvania, not one from New Jersey, not one from New York, only one from Connecticut, not one from Rhode Island, not one from New Hampshire, only one, at present, from the Massachusetts. Mr. S. Adams, Mr. Sherman, and Col. Richard Henry Lee, Mr. Chase and Mr. Paca are all that remain. The rest are dead, resigned, deserted, or cut up into governors, etc., at home." Soon Mr. Adams himself would be gone, sent by Congress as an emissary to Europe.

The Signers abandoned Congress but not the cause or public life. They had pledged their lives, and a number gambled with theirs on the battlefield—among them Lewis Morris, Rush, Rodney, Whipple, Heyward, Middleton, and Rutledge. They had pledged their honor, and nearly all continued to risk it in politics, constructing constitutions for their newly made states, serving as governors, judges, and legislators. They had pledged their fortunes, and all in varying degrees suffered for their boldness. The British looted the country mansions of Middleton, Heyward, Witherspoon, Hopkinson, and Lewis Morris. They burned Braxton's great house to the ground. Wythe lost nearly all he owned. McKean was "hunted like a fox by the enemy," he recalled after the war, "compelled to move my family five times in a few months, and at last fixed them in a little log house on the banks of the Susquehanna," only to have them there harassed by Indians. "The loss of property I treat with contempt," said Hooper, "and in this the British have struck deeper than I suspected—but the dread of my family suffering from want—Oh my God!"

After the war had ended and independence had become a reality, nearly all the Signers continued to be absorbed by politics. A few, as they looked back in their old age, wondered if their decision in 1776 had been the right one. Rush, watching America transform itself into what he called "a bedollared nation," remarked to John Adams in 1808: "I feel pain when I am reminded of my exertions in the cause of what we called liberty, and sometimes wish I could erase my name from the Declaration of Independence."

Adams instantly rebuked his friend. "You and I, in the Revolution, acted from principle. We did our duty, as we then believed, according to our best information, judgment and consciences. Shall we now repent this? God forbid! No! If a banishment to Cayenne or to Botany Bay, or even the guillotine, were to be the necessary consequences of it to us, we ought not to repent. Repent? This is impossible. How can a man repent of his virtues?"

The Declaration of Independence

July 4, 1776
The unanimous Declaration of the thirteen United States of America

W hen in the course of human events, it becomes necessary for one people to dissolve the political bands which have connected them with another, and to assume among the powers of the earth the separate and equal station to which the Laws of Nature and of Nature's God entitle them, a decent respect to the opinions of mankind requires that they should declare the causes which impel them to the separation.

We hold these truths to be self-evident, that all men are created equal, that they are endowed by their Creator with certain unalienable rights, that among these are life, liberty, and the pursuit of happiness. That to secure these rights, governments are instituted among men, deriving their just powers from the consent of the governed. That whenever any form of government becomes destructive of these ends, it is the right of the people to alter or to abolish it, and to institute new government, laying its foundation on such principles and organizing its powers in such form, as to them shall seem most likely to effect their safety and happiness. Prudence, indeed, will dictate that governments long established should not be changed for light and transient causes; and accordingly all experience hath shown, that mankind are more disposed to suffer, while evils are sufferable, than to right themselves by abolishing the forms to which they are accustomed. But when a long train of abuses and usurpations, pursuing invariably the same object evinces a design to reduce them under absolute despotism, it is their right, it is their duty, to throw off such government, and to provide new guards for their future security. Such has been the patient sufferance of these Colonies; and such is now the necessity which constrains them to alter their former systems of government. The history of the present King of Great Britain is a history of repeated injuries and usurpations, all having in direct object the establishment of an absolute tyranny over these States. To prove this, let facts be submitted to a candid world.

He has refused his assent to laws, the most wholesome and necessary for the public good.

He has forbidden his Governors to pass laws of immediate and pressing importance, unless suspended in their operation till his assent should be obtained; and when so suspended, he has utterly neglected to attend to them.

He has refused to pass other laws for the accommodation of large districts of people, unless those people would relinquish the right of representation in the legislature, a right inestimable to them and formidable to tyrants only.

He has called together legislative bodies at places unusual, uncomfortable, and distant from the depository of their public records, for the sole purpose of fatiguing them into compliance with his measures.

He has dissolved representative houses repeatedly, for opposing with manly firmness his invasions on the rights of the people.

He has refused for a long time, after such dissolutions, to cause others to be elected; whereby the legislative powers, incapable of annihilation, have returned to the people at large for their exercise; the State remaining in the meantime exposed to all the dangers of invasion from without and convulsions within.

He has endeavoured to prevent the population of these States; for that purpose obstructing the laws for naturalization of foreigners; refusing to pass others to encourage their migration hither, and raising the conditions of new appropriations of lands.

He has obstructed the administration of justice, by refusing his assent to laws for establishing judiciary powers.

He has made judges dependent on his will alone, for the tenure of their offices, and the amount and payment of their salaries.

He has erected a multitude of new offices, and sent hither swarms of officers to harass our people, and eat out their substance.

He has kept among us, in times of peace, standing armies without the consent of our legislatures.

He has affected to render the military independent of and superior to the civil power.

He has combined with others to subject us to a jurisdiction foreign to our constitution, and unacknowledged by our laws; giving his assent to their acts of pretended legislation:

For quartering large bodies of armed troops among us:

For protecting them, by a mock trial, from punishment for any murders which they should commit on the inhabitants of these States:

For cutting off our trade with all parts of the world:

For imposing taxes on us without our consent:

For depriving us in many cases of the benefits of trial by jury:

For transporting us beyond seas to be tried for pretended offences:

For abolishing the free system of English laws in a neighbouring Province, establishing therein an arbitrary government, and enlarging its boundaries so as to render it at once an example and fit instrument for introducing the same absolute rule into these Colonies:

For taking away our Charters, abolishing our most valuable laws, and altering fundamentally the forms of our governments:

For suspending our own Legislatures, and declaring themselves invested with power to legislate for us in all cases whatsoever.

He has abdicated government here, by declaring us out of his protection and waging war against us.

He has plundered our seas, ravaged our coasts, burnt our towns, and destroyed the lives of our people.

He is at this time transporting large armies of foreign mercenaries to compleat the works of death, desolation, and tyranny, already begun with circumstances of cruelty and perfidy scarcely paralleled in the most barbarous ages, and totally unworthy the head of a civilized nation.

He has constrained our fellow citizens taken captive on the high seas to bear arms against their country, to become the executioners of their friends and brethren, or to fall themselves by their hands.

He has excited domestic insurrections amongst us, and has endeavoured to bring on the inhabitants of our frontiers the merciless Indian savages, whose known rule of warfare is an undistinguished destruction of all ages, sexes, and conditions.

In every stage of these oppressions we have petitioned for redress in the most humble terms: our repeated petitions have been answered only by repeated injury. A prince whose character is thus marked by every act which may define a tyrant, is unfit to be the ruler of a free people.

Nor have we been wanting in attention to our British brethren. We have warned them from time to time of attempts by their Legislature to extend an unwarrantable jurisdiction over us. We have reminded them of the circumstances of our emigration and settlement here. We have appealed to their native justice and magnanimity, and we have conjured them by the ties of our common kindred to disavow these usurpations, which would inevitably interrupt our connections and correspondence. They too have been deaf to the voice of justice and of consanguinity. We must, therefore, acquiesce in the necessity, which denounces our separation, and hold them, as we hold the rest of mankind, enemies in war, in peace friends.

We, therefore, the Representatives of the United States of America, in General Congress assembled, appealing to the Supreme Judge of the world for the rectitude of our intentions, do, in the name, and by authority of the good people of these Colonies, solemnly publish and declare, That these United Colonies are, and of right ought to be Free and Independent States; that they are absolved from all allegiance to the British Crown, and that all political connection between them and the State of Great Britain is and ought to be totally dissolved; and that as Free and Independent States they have full power to levy war, conclude peace, contract alliances establish commerce, and to do all other acts and things which independent States may of right do. And for the support of this declaration, with a firm reliance on the protection of Divine Providence, we mutually pledge to each other our lives, our fortunes and our sacred honor.

JOHN HANCOCK.[1]

---

[1]The Declaration was first published signed only by the President of Congress and the Secretary. The other members of Congress began to affix their signatures to the engrossed copy on August 2. The signatures are grouped by states, but the names of the states are not in the original.

The Signers Grouped by States

New Hampshire
Josiah Bartlett
Wm. Whipple
Matthew Thornton

Massachusetts-Bay
Saml. Adams
John Adams
Robt. Treat Paine
Elbridge Gerry

Rhode Island
Step. Hopkins
William Ellery

Connecticut
Roger Sherman
Sam'el Huntington
Wm. Williams
Oliver Wolcott

New York
Wm. Floyd
Phil. Livingston
Frans. Lewis
Lewis Morris

Pennsylvania
Robt. Morris
Benjamin Rush
Benja. Franklin
John Morton
Geo. Clymer
Jas. Smith
Geo. Taylor
James Wilson
Geo. Ross

Delaware
Caesar Rodney

Geo. Read
Tho. M'Kean

Georgia
Button Gwinnett
Lyman Hall
Geo. Walton

Maryland
Samuel Chase
Wm. Paca
Thos. Stone
Charles Carroll
of Carrollton

Virginia
George Wythe
Richard Henry Lee
Th. Jefferson
Benja. Harrison
Ths. Nelson, Jr.

Francis Lightfoot Lee
Carter Braxton

North Carolina
Wm. Hooper
Joseph Hewes
John Penn

South Carolina
Edward Rutledge
Thos. Heyward, Junr.
Thomas Lynch, Junr.
Arthur Middleton

New Jersey
Richd. Stockton
Jno. Witherspoon
Fras. Hopkinson
John Hart
Abra. Clark

Bibliographical Note

To repeat the long bibliography appended to my earlier book *A Transaction of Free Men: The Birth and Course of the Declaration of Independence* (1964) seems senseless, although many of the works listed there have been drawn on for this book. Furthermore, I assume the average reader is not interested in consulting such specialized sources as William Duane's edition of *Extracts from the Diary of Christopher Marshall . . .* (1877) or D. R. Anderson's article "Chancellor Wythe and Parson Weems," *William and Mary Quarterly*, volume 25 (1915), pages 13–20, useful as these works were to me. Yet the reader who wants to learn more about some of the fifty-six gentlemen who signed the Declaration ought to have some guide.

To that end, I suggest he look first at the *Dictionary of American Biography* (24 volumes to date, 1917–), which contains essays on all the Signers. The essays vary in quality, but all end with a short, useful bibliographical guide to the available material on the subject. Next in importance is John

Sanderson's *Biography of the Signers of the Declaration of Independence* (4 volumes, 1823–1827). Sanderson began his project when several of the Signers were still living, and he was able to interview friends and relatives of a majority of those who had died. His essays at first glance seem little more than lengthy eulogies, but a close reading reveals that Sanderson did not hesitate to expose the flaws of his subjects when he came upon them.

Only two of the Signers—Benjamin Rush and John Adams—commented at length upon their colleagues. Rush's views are found in *The Autobiography of Benjamin Rush: His "Travels through Life," Together with His Commonplace Books for 1789–1813* (1948), edited by George W. Corner; and in *Letters of Benjamin Rush* (2 volumes, 1951), edited by Lyman H. Butterfield. Adams' tart judgments are scattered through two series of *The Adams Papers*, edited by Butterfield and others: *Adams Family Correspondence, 1761–1778* (2 volumes, 1963), and *The Diary and Autobiography of John Adams* (4 volumes, 1961). Another equally important source for contemporary opinion on the Signers is Edmund C. Cody's *Letters of the Members of the Continental Congress* (8 volumes, 1921–1936).

Index

Adams, Abigail: courted, 13–14; tea of misdelivered, 190

Adams, John (1735–1826): sketch of, 9–22; and Samuel Adams, 2, 3, 5, 191; compares colonies to fleet of horses, 10; dialogue with Jefferson, 128–29; draft of Declaration read by, 136; due for holiday, 190; effects of independence battle on health of, 189; hopes for unanimous vote on independence, 153; "how can a man repent his virtues?" 218; July 1 speech of, 152; member of committee to draw up Declaration, 125; and R. T. Paine, 84–85; pays Wolcott for spirits, 64; Rush compared to, 68–69; and sloop *Liberty*, 27; Virginia delegation puzzles, 32–33; Washington proposed as army head by, 29, 84; and Whipple, 73 *opinions of:* on Samuel Adams'

health, 205; on Carroll, 199; on chance for peace, 52; on Chase, 24, 80, 81; on Congress (1777), 217; on Dickinson, 10, 62; on foreign alliances, 207; on Franklin, 176, 177–79; on Gerry, 190; on Hancock, 25; on Harrison, 40; on Hewes, 49; on Heyward, 108; on Hopkins, 55; on Jefferson, 128–29; on Jefferson's attack on king, 182; on Jefferson's coup with Declaration, ix; on July 2, 172; on Lynches, 170, 171; on Middleton, 77–78; on Morton, 62; on R. T. Paine, 82; on patience, 9, 72; on Rush, 70; on Rutledge, 46; on "turbulent Gallicks," 198; on Whipple, 207; on Willing, 62

Adams, Samuel (1722–1803): sketch of, 2–8; and John Adams, 17; caucuses of, 10; in Congress (1777), 217; departs Congress,

on role in, 71, 72; in 1777, 217;
Sherman's role in, 60; Stockton's
treatment protested by, 142
Conway, Thomas, 199
Cornplanter, Chief, 208–209
Courts of Admiralty, 14
Cushing, Thomas, 193
Cyrmic, 99

Declaration of Independence: John
Adams offered chance to write,
128–29; John Adams on "stage
effect" of, ix; committee to draft,
52, 61, 125; committee revises,
37; Congress edits, 175, 181–84;
Congress' achievement, 183–85;
Dickinson calls "skiff made of
paper," 151–52; engrossed,
193–94; "harmonizing
sentiments" of, 183–84; Jefferson
drafts, 133–36; Jefferson's
achievement, 136–37; as loyalty
oath, 213; sent to Washington,
187–88; signers, 225–26; signing,
194; text, 219–23
deists, 103, 212–13
Delancy family, 97, 98
Delaware: creates new government,
139, 163; will protect Virginia,
156
Dickinson, John: John Adams on,
9–10, 62; anti-independence
leader, 30; and First Congress,
115; and Franklin, 179–80; July 1
speech of, 151; July 2, absent,
158; R. H. Lee corresponds with,
33; as "piddling genius," 10;
Rodney's friend, 157; and "skiff
made of paper," 184; and Wilson,
43
Duane, James, 30, 39, 74
Duché, Jacob, 7
Durham (Pa.), 117
Dutch: and smuggled tea, 28

East India Company, 27, 70, 95
Edenton (N.C.), 49

Edinburgh, 42
Ellery, William (1727–1820): sketch
of, 194–97; on Hopkins, 210; and
signing, 197–98; and Sons of
Liberty, 109
Eton, 170
Eve, O. (mill owner), 31

Fairfield (Conn.), 106
Falmouth (Portland, Me.), 20, 22
Falstaff, Sir John: Harrison
compared to, 38–39
Fauquier, Francis, 122, 130
Floyd, William (1734–1821): sketch
of, 74–76
Flynt Henry ("Father Flynt"), 16
foreign alliances: and June 7
resolutions, 35; Rutledge on, 46,
48; Whipple on, 207
Fort Dusquesne, 31
Fort Louisbourg, 212
France: Carroll in, 90, 199; and
debate on independence, 45;
disposition of awaited, 45;
Franklin in, 90; Lewis in, 99;
Rush on women in, 69–70
Franklin, Benjamin (1706–1790):
sketch of, 175–80; at Albany
Congress, 54; and Canadian
mission, 80, 200; Clymer
compared to, 94; on committee to
draft Declaration, 125; elected to
Congress, 118; Hopkinson's
friend, 149; Rush befriended by,
69–70; on shaving self, x; and
signing of Declaration, 194; son
becomes Loyalist, 123; and Stamp
Act, 69; and stolen letters, 6, 28;
travels of, 90
Franklin, Mrs. Benjamin, 43
Franklin, William: appoints
Hopkinson to council, 150;
appoints Stockton to council, 141;
ejected as governor, 139; Loyalist,
123, 177
Frederick County (Md.), 199
French and Indian War: Lewis

Litchfield (Conn.), 64
Liverpool, 159
Livingston, Philip (1716–1778): sketch of, 96–98
Livingston, Robert R., Sr.: on independence, 98
Livingston, Robert R., 96; on committee to draft Declaration, 125
Livingston, William, 96, 98; elected governor, 142
Locke, John: and Declaration, 134–35
London Coffee House, 188, 189
Londonberry (N.H.), 212
Long Island: Floyd, native of, 74; Sherman on defeat of army there, 57
Loudoun County (Va.), 101
Lower Counties. See Delaware
Lovell, James, 64
Loyalists, 123, 169, 177, 209
Lynch, Thomas, Sr., 162, 163, 170, 171, 180
Lynch, Thomas, Jr. (1749–1779): sketch of, 170–71; signs Declaration, 198; as typical southerner, 108; vote for independence, 170

McKean, Thomas (1734–1817): sketch of, 214–15; "hunted like a fox," 218; on Parliament's power, 111; on Read's vote for independence, 162–63; and Rodney, 155, 157; Rush works with, 71; at Stamp Act Congress, 98, 157; votes for independence, 160
McNair, Andrew (doorkeeper), 30
Madeira wine: Hancock favors importation of, 29; Harrison partial to, 38; Ross loves, 114
Maine, 83, 212
Marblehead (Mass.), 191, 192
marine committee: Bartlett on, 104; Hopkins on, 54; Livingston on,

98; Sherman on, 60; Whipple on, 207
Marshall, John, 120
Maryland: border disputes of, 165; changes delegation's instructions, 80–81; and constitution (1776), 79
Massachusetts: Samuel Adams would have govern United States, 3; Hooper on, 167, 168
Meredith, Elizabeth. See Clymer, Mrs. George
Middle Temple: Heyward attends, 108; Lynch, Jr., attends, 170; Middleton attends, 76; Rutledge attends, 47
Middleton, Arthur (1742–1787): sketch of, 76–78; gadfly, 53, 81, 85; house looted, 218; in Italy, 90; leaves Congress, 101; as typical southerner, 108
Middleton, Mrs. Arthur, 77
Middleton, Henry, 47, 76, 77
Milford (Conn.), 81
Milton, John, 55
mobs: John Adams on, 20; Samuel Adams on when legitimate, 5, 192; and Chase's father, 78; in Marblehead, 192; in Newport, 197. See also Boston Massacre and Boston Tea Party
Monticello, 127, 131, 132
Morris, Gouverneur, 208
Morris, Lewis (1726–1798): sketch of, 208–11; house looted, 218
Morris, Robert (1734–1806): sketch of, 158–60; and Harrison, 39; and Hooper, 169; and Penn, 73, 112–113, 114; and Rodney, 157; signs Declaration, 198; and Walton, 119
Morris, Mrs. Robert, 159
Morrisania, 209
Morton, John (c. 1724–1777): sketch of, 61–63
Morven Manor, 140